GENERATIVE CONSULTING

Tools for creativity, consciousness and collective transformation

Strategy Group

Dilts Strategy Group

P. O. Box 67448

Scotts Valley CA 95067

USA

Phone: (831) 438-8314

E-Mail: info@diltstrategygroup.com

Homepage: http://www.diltstrategygroup.com

Library of Congress Control Number: 2020917247

I.S.B.N. 978-1-947629-42-4

GENERATIVE CONSULTING

Tools for creativity, consciousness and collective transformation

Robert B. Dilts

Elisabeth Falcone

Mickey A. Feher

Colette Normandeau

Jean-François Thiriet

Kathrin M. Wyss

Design and illustrations: Antonio Meza

Praise for Generative Consulting

The SFM mindset, models and toolbox are one of the most powerful I have seen as a consultant. Working with Generative Consulting is a huge advantage for the future.

Magnus Kull, Sweden
Author, trainer, senior consultant at coach2coach

Every year that advances we are deeper into the complexity of the world, a context to which we haven't been trained to deal with. However there are ways, collective ways indeed through which we can prompt ourselves and companies to better deal with uncertainty. Rigid procedures are no longer useful in this VUCA world. We need criteria and responsible freedom to learn at each step, to learn with intention and methodology. This is what Generative Consulting can provide us.

Tiago Petreca, Brazil
Founder of Kuratore and author of *Do Mindset as Mindflow (DVS)*

The Generative Consulting Method is an intelligent holistic way to approach, structure and lead a transformation process. It includes and combines the why, the how and the what in a systemic as well as very pragmatic way. It is a method that - when it comes to effective transformation - really makes a difference, that makes a difference.

Beate Weber von Koslowski, Germany
Head of Academy and Senior Consultant at permitto gmbh

I was honored to be among the first participants on the Generative Consulting program…. The entire experience was inspirational and, since graduating, I have utilized many of the models, which were flexible enough to be adapted to my own work. The SFM principles in particular have been a solid framework upon which to develop new notions of collective intelligence within the workplace – even more relevant recently, in our global, post COVID world, where remote working requires a spectacular attention to community, collaboration and collective energy – whilst recognizing the immense challenges of enormous economic stress and profound change.

It was a great experience and one which I believe has been of direct benefit to me in the development of my work as a leader in my field."

Colin Payne, UK
Vice President | Global Lead NextGen FS, Capgemini Invent

TABLE OF CONTENTS

TABLE OF CONTENTS

TABLE OF CONTENTS

Acknowledgments

We want to begin by acknowledging the late John Dilts, who co-created the Success Factor Modeling methodology with Robert. His spirit of creativity, curiosity and commitment to helping individuals and ventures reach their highest potential is at the foundation of the generative consulting approach.

It is also with great gratitude that we acknowledge Stephen Gilligan, who co-created with Robert the principles and underlying processes of generative change (starting from a generative state, accessing multiple intelligences, including all parts of the "holon," integrating multiple perspectives, etc.) that are applied throughout this book. Stephen and Robert's work with generative coaching is a powerful complement to the consulting approach described in these pages.

In addition, we would like to acknowledge the key contributions of our colleague and collaborator Antonio Meza. Antonio's illustrations are a powerful example of using multiple intelligences to bring concepts and ideas alive. We deeply appreciate Antonio's talent, effort and flexibility in bringing a completely unique style of illustration to this work. Antonio is also responsible for the overall design and layout of these pages.

We want to extend our appreciation to Tony Nutley, The Food, Agriculture and Forestry Commission of French Guyana and the others who are mentioned in the case examples for the coming chapters (several who are not named explicitly for reasons of confidentiality).

We also want to express our gratitude to the practitioners of generative change who have used the methods and given us generous feedback. It has been a valuable contribution to developing this work.

Finally, we would like to acknowledge Aimée LeBreton who did the challenging job of proofreading this book. Her input has helped to make our diversity of voices more consistent and coherent.

Robert, Elisabeth, Colette, Jean-François, Mickey and Kathrin

About this Book
Message from the authors

This book is about helping organizations to achieve something new and different from what they have before. This means that the teams and individuals who make up those organizations have to do something that is new and different from what they have done before. And to help them to do that, we, as change agents, need to think and act in new and different ways. This is the essence of generativity.

In this book, we present a unique approach to managing organizational change based on the principles and practices of Success Factor Modeling (SFM™) – a methodology for identifying the key success factors that drive effective performance. The core processes and models of SFM are detailed in the three-volume series by Robert Dilts:

* *Success Factor Modeling Volume I: Next Generation Entrepreneurs – Live Your Dreams and Make a Better World Through Your Business*

* *Success Factor Modeling Volume II: Generative Collaboration – Releasing the Creative Power of Collective Intelligence*

* *Success Factor Modeling Volume III: Conscious Leadership and Resilience – Orchestrating Innovation and Fitness for the Future*

A number of these volumes have been translated into other languages including German, French, Spanish, Italian, Chinese, Russian, Korean and Farsi. The Success Factor Modeling approach has also sparked a number of other projects which have culminated in books such as *MasterMind Groups: Accelerators of Success* and *The PERICEO Tool: Teams and Organizations, Develop Your Capacity for Collective Intelligence.*

In the following pages, we will show how consultants and business leaders can apply this approach to take their clients, teams and ventures to a new level of functioning and achievement.

The *we* voice that we use in this book stands for the SFM Leadership Team – an international group of people who have been working intimately together since 2015 to bring the vision, principles and tools of Success Factor Modeling and Generative Consulting to entrepreneurs and organizations throughout the world. The core SFM Leadership Team members[1] who authored this book are Colette Normandeau, from Quebec, Canada, Jean-François Thiriet and Elisabeth Falcone, from France, Mickey A. Feher, a Hungarian living in New York, Kathrin M. Wyss, a Swiss German living in the San Francisco Bay Area and SFM co-creator Robert Dilts, from the Silicon Valley area. Each of us has many years' experience in consulting, coaching and training.

This *Generative Consulting* book is the fruit of a truly collaborative team effort. We each spearheaded one chapter as an individual author or in a small team, writing from our experience and in our own style, and sharing how we applied SFM models and tools to foster generative change with clients. We show how organizational change agents can enrich their current methods by adding the unique principles and distinctions encompassed by the generative change approach, in order to develop new solutions to different types of challenges.

During our writing process, we asked ourselves, "What exactly makes this approach so generative, unique and important to share with readers?" All the chapters were reviewed by each team member using the following set of questions to make sure that the content was as valuable and practical as possible for our readers:

---

1   http://diltsstrategygroup.com/DSG/LeadershipTeam.html.

a. What would I, as a consultant, want to know about what was done to make a "generative" difference?

   i. What am I still curious about at the end of the chapter?

   ii. What do I have yet to understand and what am I missing, as a generative consultant?

b. How are the core generative consulting components – including multiple intelligences, the seven-step SFM DIAMOND Model and the nine generative consulting competences – applied in the chapter's case examples?

c. How will readers use the content as generative consultants or business leaders?

d. How practical is this chapter?

Our last chapter (Chapter 6 *Being the Generative Change*) is based on a live conversation that we held in November 2019 to reflect on what inspires our work and how we apply it with our clients. We also reflected on the personal qualities, skills and mindset necessary to effectively apply the SFM methodology as consultants or business leaders.

We hope that you find this book to be both practical and inspirational and that you try out this approach with your clients, teams and ventures to spark them to a new level of performance and achievement. It is our aspiration to support organizations – from start-up ventures to multinational corporations – to identify their strengths and areas for improvement and to apply SFM and generative change tools and practices in order to attain a strong, sustainable and socially responsible state of growth and profitability.

More information about Success Factor Modeling and generative change in businesses is available in other books and training programs conducted around the world by authorized SFM practitioners and trainers. We are also building an online community that you can join by subscribing to our newsletter through the Dilts Strategy Group website at www.diltsstrategygroup.com.

We look forward to introducing you and welcoming you to this exciting community.

The authors

Robert, Elisabeth, Colette, Jean-François, Mickey and Kathrin.

Rational thinking, even assisted by any conceivable electronic computers, cannot predict the future. All it can do is to map out the probability space as it appears at the present and which will be different tomorrow when one of the infinity of possible states will have materialized. Technological and social inventions are broadening this probability space all the time; it is now incomparably larger than it was before the Industrial Revolution — for good or for evil.

The future cannot be predicted, but futures can be invented. It was man's ability to invent which has made human society what it is. The mental processes of inventions are still mysterious. They are rational but not logical, that is to say, not deductive.

— Dennis Gabor (inventor of the hologram), 1963

Chapter 1
Overview of Generative Consulting

Robert B. Dilts

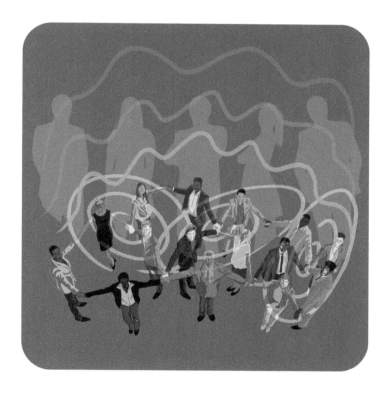

1.1 What does a consultant do?

In general, a consultant (from Latin: *consultare,* "to deliberate") is a professional who provides businesses or organizations with expert advice in a particular area. *Internal consultants* operate within an organization and are available to be consulted on their areas of specialization by other departments or individuals (acting as clients). *External consultants* are employed from outside an organization (either by a consulting firm or as independent contractors) and provide their expertise on a temporary basis for a fee.

Consultants provide advice to their clients in a variety of ways, most often in the form of reports or presentations. In some specialized fields, a consultant may develop customized software or other products for clients. Depending on the nature of their consulting services and the wishes of their clients, the consultants' advice may be made public or kept private.

Usually, a consultant has an area of expertise that an organization or a team need to reach a desired outcome. Hence, people who hire a consultant are primarily looking for some kind of advice to solve a problem or make a change. They are paying for the consultant's expertise in a specific area so that they can better achieve a particular result.

1.2 What is the difference between traditional consulting and coaching?

The term "consulting" can refer to a wide range of activities that overlap both coaching and counseling. Coaching derives from a sports training model and encourages individuals to improve their performance through the development of their personal resources and abilities. A coach operates primarily through a conversation with an individual or, in some cases, a team. By asking key questions, coaches help their clients define specific goals, identify the resources they need and establish a plan of action to achieve their goals. Counseling involves a more therapeutic approach, which focuses on problem solving and remedial change to address particular problems and symptoms.

In contrast with coaches and counselors who work mostly on a one-to-one basis with their clients, a consultant must take a broader perspective. A consultant not only works with an individual client but also with the larger system of that client's organization which the client seeks to impact. In other words, coaching and counseling focus on personal development while consulting focuses primarily on organizational development. Effective consulting requires the ability to understand the key dynamics of an organization and to offer advice about how to influence those dynamics. To do this, a consultant must frequently integrate goal setting and planning with problem solving.

One of the main differences between coaching and consulting is the time frame typically involved. A complete coaching session may be done in a half-an-hour to an hour, depending on a client's readiness. A consulting project can take days, weeks or even months. A consultant might need to spend a whole day or many hours on any one issue.

One of the reasons for this difference in time frame is because consulting needs to address a larger and more complex system of people and events than coaching. In coaching, the focus is on the specific individual facing the coach. In consulting, the focus minimally involves working with a specific individual and his or her team. It may also include the team's division or department and, potentially, the whole organization and its marketplace.

1.3 What is generative consulting, and how is it different than traditional consulting?

Traditionally, businesses and organizations focus on achieving concrete, clearly definable results. While this is necessary to be successful, it can narrow one's scope of imagination. In fact, one of the major challenges for companies and organizations is the ability to innovate, create or generate something new. This ability to generate new opportunities as well as to produce practical results is the emphasis of generative consulting.

To "generate" means to create something that has not previously existed. The focus of "generative change" is to cultivate creativity: in teams, ventures, relationships and individuals. The goal of *generative consulting*, in particular, is to help teams and organizations evolve and function in ways that are both new and more effective. To accomplish this, a generative consultants develops a programs or paths for their clients, combining multiple interventions in order to reach achieve completely new key organizational outcomes.

When working in situations that are completely new or unprecedented, it is not possible to use "off- the- shelf" solutions that have worked in the past. Consultants and their client organizations must have a fundamental problem-solving structure that allows them to identify the key issues and the resources needed for change.

When organizations are going where no one has ever been before, there is no "content expert." No one has previously accomplished what needs to be done and no one already knows the way. In such situations, expertise has to be at a process level – the process of assisting people to create something completely new.

Thus, the emphasis of generative consulting is on process rather than content. That is, consultants do not need to be "content experts." Instead, consultants guide people through processes which help them to maximize their own resources and use their imaginations to come up with creative options. As Albert Einstein famously said: "Imagination is more important than knowledge." He pointed out that knowledge can only tell us about what already exists and not what could be, should be or will be.

Generative consulting often requires introducing a whole new mindset into an organization. As we will explore later on, this new mindset includes cognitive understanding but also involves engaging other forms of intelligence, such as somatic intelligence, emotional intelligence and collective intelligence.

Because organizations are made of people, organizational development must also be supported by people development. To take an organization to a new level, individuals and teams must operate at a new level. This is where coaching and consulting overlap to some degree in generative change. The common connection between generative coaching and generative consulting is empowerment. That is always the ultimate goal – people are more empowered to co-create a world to which they want to belong.

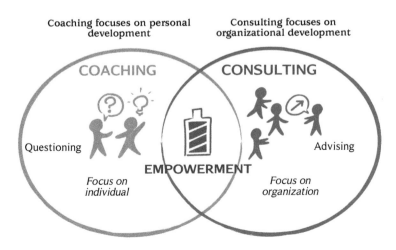

The Relationship between Coaching and Consulting

1.4 The Building Blocks of Generative Consulting

The process of generative consulting brings together a unique and powerful set of building blocks:

* Based on the fundamental principles and premises of generative change, generative consulting methodology is organized around a *seven-step generative consulting process*.

* The implementation of the steps is supported by *nine core generative consulting competences*.

* The seven steps of generative consulting are applied to the *three critical areas of business success* that most require generative solutions: *stimulating growth, surviving crisis and managing transition*.

* Depending on the type of situation, the generative consulting process applies *key models* drawn from the application of Success Factor Modeling to next-generation entrepreneurship, collective intelligence and conscious leadership and resilience.

GENERATIVE CONSULTING METHODOLOGY

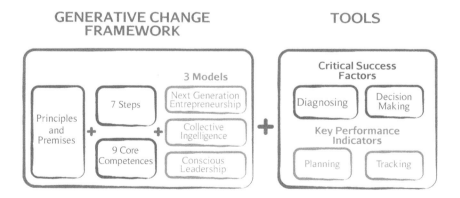

Overview of Generative Consulting Methodology

We will summarize the different facets of generative consulting in a structure that we refer to as the Success Factor Modeling (SFM) DIAMOND Model, which will present at the end of this chapter.

In addition to the steps, competences and models listed earlier, generative consulting applies particular tools. Some tools are meant for *diagnosis* and *decision making* processes that are based on critical success factors (CSFs). Other tools are for *planning* and for *tracking progress*, which relate to key performance indicators (KPIs) used to indicate whether the consulting intervention is making any difference or not.

For generative change to truly work, these tools often have to be created. They do not preexist, so these key performance indicators and the tools with which to measure them have to be collectively defined.

1.5 Principles of Generative Change

Any type of generative change, including generative consulting interventions, emphasize the importance of working within a "generative state." Technically speaking, this has to do with the state of our mental attitude and perceptual "filters." At an interpersonal level, these filters relate to the way we use our bodies (somatic and emotional intelligence), our brains (cognitive intelligence) and our interactions with others (relational and "field" intelligence) when addressing a goal or problem.

One of the main functions of a generative state is to move from a place where there is only one meaning and one possibility regarding some situation to a place where whatever is happening can be perceived as having many different possible expressions and meanings. The first step in any creative process is to enter an open state of mind (the "dreamer" state), where something can be perceived as a process with the potential for many different expressions instead of as a fixed form that is either positive or negative. The expression which is the most appropriate for the particular situation to be addressed can then be chosen (the "realist" phase).

One way to talk about generative change would be in terms of the dynamics between the "quantum world" and the "classical world" in physics. The quantum world is essentially "a field of infinite possibilities" encompassing all the possible forms which something could take. The classical world is made up of a single particular ongoing, concrete expression of all those possibilities.

To be truly generative, change needs to start in the non-classical, non-physical quantum field of many possibilities (the "dreamer" state). Those possibilities are then adapted to both the opportunities and constraints of an existing situation (the "realist" phase). Lastly, adjustments and updates must be made to ensure the new conditions are appropriate and sustainable (the "critic" stage).

Therefore, generative change work involves setting a direction or intention, entering a generative state and then moving into some type of action and execution – moving from what we would call the "quantum world of possibilities" to the classical world of concrete expression. This movement invariably brings up obstacles and interferences that must be addressed and resolved in order to continue to progress in the direction of the original intention.

One of the challenges of generative change is that, because an individual, team or organization must go somewhere new, and there are many possibilities, the details of the new destination are not usually clear at the beginning. So the desired change needs to be initially defined more as a *direction* rather than a precise destination. As an analogy, if you are exploring uncharted territory without any preexisting maps, you need to navigate by using a compass and the stars as guides. Similarly, generative consulting often involves creating and applying a different or more expanded set of key performance indicators than traditional consulting.

To accomplish this with respect to a complex and dynamic situation, a generative consultant needs to gather and organize a lot of information and then organize that information in some way. A big challenge is that this process requires so much left-brain capacity that the consultant can start to lose the connections with the body, with the heart and our other intelligences. Effective consulting requires a high level of intellect and brain work, as well as a lot of information gathering and information organizing skills. But it equally involves as much somatic intelligence, emotional intelligence and relational intelligence. Where companies often have biggest problems is leaving out the importance of somatic, emotional and relational (or "field") intelligence.

1.6 Using Multiple Intelligences

To be generative, you cannot simply work with verbal information and numbers. In generative consulting, we bring together multiple intelligences as a way to support greater understanding and to inspire new ideas and solutions. The basic principle of multiple intelligences is that, *the more ways you have to understand something, the more you understand it*. If you only have a mathematical or monetary way of understanding something, your understanding is limited. If, however, in addition you have a metaphorical, a somatic way and a visual way, you understand it more completely. The purpose of generative consulting is to represent something in multiple ways. In generative consulting, we very often work with somatic representations, images and metaphors in combination with traditional verbal language.

When clients are defining their direction and intention for change, for instance, in addition to requesting a verbal description of the desired state, a generative consultant may also ask for a visual image. The consultant might ask the client, "What is your mental picture for that desired state? What image do you see?" Rather than describe the image in words, the consultant may ask clients to draw what they see on a piece of paper or white board. These visual images are more effective than words for bringing out the interrelationships between the key elements of change. Verbal representations come more from the "left-brain" and focus more on objects and sequencing while visual representations are generated by the "right-brain" and emphasize patterns and relationships. Incorporating color into the images can bring out a whole different level of dynamics.

One of the other essential areas of intelligence necessary to promote generative change is the intelligence of the body; what we call "somatic intelligence." In generative consulting, for every key piece of cognitive information you gather, it is also useful to get a "somatic model." Let's say that a company is in a state of inertia; the consultant may ask clients to "Show that inertia with your body. What is a movement or gesture that characterizes what is going on?" The generative consultant would then say, "Now, show the desired state with your body. What would be different?" This often brings greater insight into what is going on than a lot of verbalization. Similarly, if a team is in conflict about making a decision, a generative consultant might say, "Show the conflict with your body. What is a somatic model of the conflict? Now, demonstrate with your body what needs to change and what would be the result?" Somatic representations tend to more effectively capture more effectively than words the relational and emotional "fields" related to a situation than words.

Using multiple intelligences to communicate
in a generative way

We will also frequently use metaphors as a way to gather and organize information in generative coaching. Systems theorist Gregory Bateson pointed out that "everything is a metaphor for everything else." A car is a metaphor for a company. A family is a metaphor for a car and a company. A forest is a metaphor for a company and a car. Every system is a metaphor for every other system. A basketball team is a metaphor for an executive committee. An executive committee is a metaphor for an orchestra. An orchestra is a metaphor for the process of product development and so on. Any system can provide information about any other system. A generative consultant might ask: "What is a metaphor or analogy for the change that the company needs to make? What is your metaphor for its present state? The current state of the organization is like ... what?" Metaphors often require and combine both left-brain and right-brain thinking

1.7 The COACH State

To maintain access to all the necessary types of intelligence, a major focus of the generative consulting process is for both the consultant and the clients to constantly cultivate an inner state characterized by the acronym COACH (see *SFM Vol. I*, pp. 34-35 and *SFM Vol. II*I, pp. 64-67), which is:

* **C**entered in yourself, especially in the "gut" (your belly center)

* **O**pen to new information, ideas and possibilities

* **A**ttentive to what is going on within and around you with awareness and mindfulness

* **C**onnected to yourself, your resources and to the larger system(s) of which you are a part

* **H**olding whatever is happening from a mindset of creativity and curiosity (hospitality)

The COACH State is the foundation for a generative state. The opposite of this occurs when we one collapses into an inner stuck state that can be summarized by the letters CRASH:

* **C**ontraction
* **R**eactivity
* **A**nalysis Paralysis
* **S**eparation
* **H**ostility

When we "CRASH," we lose our connection to our creative imagination and other inner resources, and everything becomes more difficult. When we confront an outer obstacle from the CRASH state, we experience it as an unsolvable problem.

Being able to achieve and maintain the COACH state, especially in difficult and challenging circumstances, is one of the most important goals of generative consulting. Generative consultants constantly work to remain in this state themselves and ensure that every key player in the change process can think and act from this state.

1.8 Holons, Holarchies and Holograms

One of the major challenges of generative consulting is to be able to set a direction and define necessary changes involving all the key players: the client, the team, the organization's relevant roles, departments or divisions and, at times, the organizational culture. Thus, another key skill of generative consulting is cultivating the capacity for thinking in terms of "holons" and "holarchies."

It is an intriguing reality of our Human existence that, on the one hand, we are whole and independent beings; and on the other hand, we are also part of systems bigger than us. Author and political philosopher Arthur Koestler used the term "holarchy" to describe the dynamics of this relationship. In *The Act of Creation* (1964, p. 287), Koestler explained:

> *A living organism or social body is not an aggregation of elementary particles or elementary processes; it is an integrated hierarchy of semiautonomous sub-wholes, consisting of sub-sub-wholes, and so on. Thus the functional units on every level of the hierarchy are double-faced as it were: they act as whole when facing downwards, as parts when facing upwards.*

In other words, something that integrates parts at the level below into a larger whole becomes a part itself of the level above it. Water, for instance, is a unique entity that emerges from the bonding of hydrogen and oxygen. Water itself, however, can become a part of many other larger entities, from orange juice to oceans to the human body. Thus, water is both a whole made up of smaller parts and a part of other larger wholes.

In *A Brief History of Everything* (1996), transformational teacher and author Ken Wilber described this relationship in the following way:

> *Arthur Koestler coined the term "holon" to refer to an entity that is itself a whole and simultaneously a part of some other whole. And if you start to look closely at the things and processes that actually exist, it soon becomes obvious that they are not merely wholes, they are also parts of something else. They are whole/parts, they are holons.*
>
> *For instance, a whole atom is part of a whole molecule, and the whole molecule is part of the whole cell, and the whole cell is part of a whole organism, and so on. Each of these entities is neither a whole nor a part, but a whole/part, a holon.*

According to Wilber, each new whole includes, yet transcends the parts at the level below it. It is important to point out that if a lower level in a holarchy is not present, the levels above it will not be fully expressed. The lower levels are the necessary components of all higher levels.

Each of us is thus a holon. We are made up of whole atoms, which make up whole molecules that combine to create whole cells, which in turn join together to make whole tissues, whole organs and whole interconnected nervous systems from which our whole body is formed. We in turn are part of progressively larger wholes: a family, a professional community and the whole system of living creatures on this planet, which is, in turn, part of our solar system and, ultimately, the whole universe.

Generative Consulting Views Each Person and Organization as a "Holon"

In generative change and generative consulting, the notion of holon is crucial. When we work with individuals, groups or organizations, we consider them as part of a holarchy. They are an independent whole, but they are also made up of other wholes and are part of larger wholes. The concept of holon is so very critical in organizations, because there are many different wholes to be worked with – whole teams are parts of whole divisions, which are parts of a whole geographic area, and so on. One division may be in the United States, and another may be in France, and another, in China, etc. So, a holon awareness is absolutely necessary.

Parallel to the concept of holon is the dynamic of holographic coding: each part of a holon contains the whole and can recreate it. An example of this principle is the human body. The DNA for the whole body is in each of its cells. Therefore, any cell of the body can recreate the whole body (this is the principle at the basis of "cloning").

In organizations this is very obvious. Each member of the organization is both a part of and a representative of the entire organization. If the members of an organization (especially key members) do not share basic common values and have a common intention, chaos comes quickly and mistakes happen quite easily. So, the "whole" has to be in every part. This representation of the whole (the organization's DNA) takes the form of its vision, mission and values. If these are not shared, cultivated and implemented by every member of the organization, then these kinds of cancer-like activities occur, where the part is no longer part of the whole. It is separate and acting only on its own behalf.

Thus, the idea of holon is key in generative consulting. We are made up of other wholes – whole organs which are made up of cells, which in turn are made up of molecules, atoms, etc. We are also part of bigger larger wholes – a family, a professional community, a culture, a planet, and so on. As soon as any part of the holon becomes neglected, there will be predictable problems.

A good example is a U.K. company that was started by a group of seven people. On the surface, the business was very successful financially and growing very quickly. However, within the first two years of operations, two of the founders got cancer, two got divorced and one had a breakdown. Obviously, this is not a sustainable situation.

If we do not take care of our physical health, there will be predictable problems. If we leave out attending to our families, there are will be predictable problems. Similarly, phenomena like global warming and climate change are also the results of our disregarding aspects of the larger holon in which we are operating.

Attending to the entire holon is crucial for successful and sustainable change; and it is really difficult to do. When people are starting their own business and fighting for survival, they are not thinking about the whole holarchy. They are not necessarily thinking about the planet, about their health or perhaps being attentive to their family's needs, and so on. In fact, a key part of a consultant's job is to remind clients that this holarchy is there and needs to be considered when decisions are made and actions are taken.

This is where *aesthetic intelligence* is especially significant in generative consulting. Aesthetic intelligence is the basis of harmony, beauty and balance. It involves sensitivity to how different parts of something (such as music, painting, food, architecture, dance, etc.) relate to one another and to the larger whole. Complex and dynamic organizations have many interacting parts and a number of areas where things can get out of harmony and balance. Identifying and addressing these areas of imbalance and disharmony requires that consultants and clients represent and reflect upon as much of the holon as possible. To be effective, this cannot be done in an abstract, intellectual manner, but instead in a way that allows them to find where and at what level there is disharmony or imbalance and what is causing it. This is one of the key contributions of Success Factor Modeling.

1.9 Success Factor Modeling™

One of the things that distinguishes generative consulting from all the other types of consulting is its incorporation of the *Success Factor Modeling*™ (SFM) framework. Success Factor Modeling™ is a methodology originally developed by Robert and John Dilts to identify, understand and apply the critical success factors that drive and support exceptional performance in people, groups and organizations. It explores and identifies *the differences that make a difference* between exceptional, average and poor performance of various types.

Success Factor Modeling™ is founded upon a set of principles and distinctions which are uniquely suited to analyze and distinguish crucial patterns of *business practices* and *behavioral skills* used by effective individuals, teams and organizations to achieve their desired outcomes. The SFM™ process is used to discern key characteristics and capabilities shared by outstanding entrepreneurs, teams and business leaders in order to define specific models, tools and skills that can be used by others to greatly increase their chances of producing impact and achieving success.

Thus, the objective of the Success Factor Modeling™ process is to create an *instrumental map* supported by a variety of exercises, formats and tools that allow people to apply the factors that have been modeled in order to achieve key outcomes within their chosen context. To accomplish this, SFM applies the following basic template:

The Basic Success Factor Modeling Template

Our *mindset*—which is made up of our inner state, attitude and thinking processes—produces outer behavioral *actions*. It is our mindset that determines what we do and the type of actions we take in particular situations. These actions, in turn, create *outcomes* in the external world. Thus, achieving desired outcomes in our environment requires the proper mindset to produce the necessary and appropriate actions.

According to SFM, all successful change requires a change in mindset. It is our mindset that determines what we do. And it is what we do that determines the outcomes we achieve.

We can make a useful analogy with a computer. You can't expect computers to do something different if you don't change the software they are running. You can't tell the computers, "You should be doing something different," and then run the same programs. You've got to change the programming to change the behavior of the computers. That, in turn, will change the results that you're getting.

At its foundation, all consulting is essentially directed toward supporting clients to achieve some desired outcome – whether it is to grow, manage a crisis, make a transition, optimize its performance in some areas, etc. Whether or not an outcome is achieved is a consequence of the actions taken by the members of the organization. In generative consulting, it is assumed that changes in actions and the achievement of organizational outcomes are a function of a shift in mindset that has to happen in order for changes in performance to take place. A major shift in mindset is especially necessary in order to create something new.

Watch your thoughts, they become words.
Watch your words, they become actions.
Watch your actions, they become habits.
Watch your habits, they become character.
Watch your character, it becomes your destiny.
-- Lao Tzu

1.10 Key Levels of Success Factors

Success Factor Modeling identifies several levels of factors that contribute to a successful performance.

* **Environmental** factors determine the external opportunities or constraints which individuals and organizations must recognize and to which they must react to reach their desired outcomes. They involve considering *where* and *when* success occurs.

* **Behavioral** factors are the specific actions taken to achieve success. They involve *what*, specifically, must be done or accomplished to succeed.

* **Capabilities** relate to the mental maps, plans or strategies that lead to success. They direct *how* actions are selected and monitored.

* **Beliefs and values** provide the reinforcement that supports or inhibits particular capabilities and actions. They relate to *why* a particular path is taken and the deeper motivations which drive people to act or persevere.

* **Identity** factors relate to people's sense of role or mission. These factors are a function of *who* individuals or groups perceive themselves to be.

* **Purpose** relate to people's view of the larger system of which they are a part. These factors involve for *whom* or for *what* a particular path or course of action has been taken. In a business, this usually relates to its customers, shareholders and team.

Environment and behavior have to do with the outcomes we are trying to achieve and the actions needed to reach them. That is the foundation, or "bottom line" of a consulting intervention. According to SFM, if we want to do things differently and get different results, we need to engage different know-how and capabilities. In order to do something new and different, it is necessary to get into a generative mindset.

To make changes in mindset a priority, they must be supported by particular beliefs and values which provide the motivation to develop and apply new capabilities. Our beliefs and values select and support the capabilities that we will engage. We develop and use certain capabilities, because we believe they are needed in a particular situation.

Our sense of identity is another very significant factor making up our mindset. Identity encompasses and organizes the other aspects that make up our mindset. Most crises, areas of growth and transitions will require a significant change in behavior. Most of them will require new capabilities. Some will require a shift in values and beliefs, i.e. a shift in priorities and organizational focus. Some, however, will require a shift in corporate identity. Those will bring some of the biggest changes.

As an example of identity shift, *Apple, Inc.* used to be called *Apple Computer*. Today, however, most of their revenue is not directly related to computers. It comes from smart phones, tablets, on-line music, etc. This is an example of an identity shift. They renamed the company from Apple Computer to Apple Inc. to acknowledge that their identity was no longer just a computer company.

An even deeper level of change would be related to an organization's vision and purpose, or reason for being. This relates to issues such as, "What is the fundamental nature of the venture? Who are its customers and what is the venture's vision for how it serves those customers?"

1.11 Balancing "Ego" and "Soul"

Combining the concepts of holons and holarchies with the various levels of success factors creates a powerful matrix from which to view the dynamics of individuals, teams and organizations. According to this matrix, our lives and motivations are driven by two complementary aspects of our identities: those emerging from (1) our existence as a separate, independent whole, and those arising from (2) our existence as a part of a larger whole (e.g., family, profession, community, etc.). The part of our existence that we experience as an individual whole we typically call our "ego." The part of our existence that we experience as a holon (part of a larger whole) can be referred to as our "soul."

Our *ego* has to do with the development and preservation of our sense of being a separate self, perceiving reality from our own independent and isolated perspective. At the level of environment, the ego tends to focus on dangers and constraints, and on the pursuit of short-term gain and pleasure. Consequently, at the level of behavior, the ego tends to be more reactive to external conditions. The capabilities associated with the ego are generally those connected with the conscious cognitive intellect, such as analysis and strategy. At the level of beliefs and values, the ego focuses on safety, security, approval, control, achievement and self-benefit. A sense of permission is typically needed to engage fully in some activity: the sense that one should, should not, needs to or must not do something. At the identity level, the ego relates to our social roles and who we feel we should be or need to be in order to obtain approval or acknowledgment. At the level of spirit or purpose, the ego is oriented toward survival, recognition and ambition.

Our *soul* has to do with our sense of belonging, contribution and service to something larger than ourselves. At the level of environment, the soul tends to focus on opportunities for expression and contribution. As a result, at the level of behavior the soul tends to respond more proactively to external conditions. The capabilities associated with the soul are generally those related to the perception and expression of energy and emotional intelligence. At the level of beliefs and values, the soul focuses on internal motivations such as service, contribution, connection, being, expansion and awakening. At the identity level, the soul relates to our mission and the unique gifts that we bring into the world. At the level of spirit or purpose, the soul is focused on our vision of what we want to create in the world through us, but that is in service of something beyond us.

From the perspective of Success Factor Modeling, both ego and soul are necessary for a healthy and successful existence. The primary questions relating to our ego are about what we want to achieve for ourselves in terms of ambition and role: "What type of life do I want to create for myself?" and "What type of person do I need to be in order to create the life I want?" These are about living out our dreams for ourselves. The primary questions with respect to the soul are those related to our vision and mission for the larger systems of which we are a part: "What do I want to create in the world through me that is in service of something beyond me?" and "What is my unique contribution to bringing that vision into expression?"

In the SFM approach, these distinctions of ego (one's self as an independent whole) and soul (ourselves as holons that are a part of a larger system) are combined with the various levels of success factors, as shown in the following diagram.

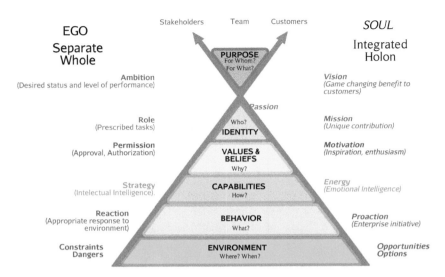

**Levels of Success Factors Relating to "Ego" and "Soul"
in Individuals and Organizations.**

The complementary dimensions of ego and soul tend to bring out a different emphasis for each level of success factors. The ego side accentuates ambition, role, the importance of permission, strategy and appropriate reactions to constraints and potential dangers in the environment. The soul side places priority on vision, mission, inner motivation and activating the energy and emotional intelligence needed to proactively take advantage of environmental opportunities.

Research with Success Factor Modeling indicates that the most generative performance of an individual, a team or an organization occurs when the levels of success factors related to both ego and soul are balanced, aligned and integrated. In contrast, conflict between the factors related to ego and soul are responsible for much of the struggle and failure experienced by individuals, teams and organizations.

1.12 Ego and Soul in Organizations

The dynamics between ego and soul operates in a similar way within a company or organization. The ego of the organization is made up of the owners and shareholders, whose concern is with survival, profitability (the "bottom line") and return on investment. Organizations and their members reflect this concern in their ambition regarding status and level of performance.

The soul of an organization lies in the value that it provides for customers and the larger social and physical environment. This value is created by the vision of the organization and the unique contribution and mission of the organization and its members with respect to the larger systems which it serves.

Team members and employees clearly operate in the middle of the two dimensions of ego and soul. They need to find the right balance between their responsibilities to both shareholders and customers in order to effectively do their jobs and serve their purposes.

When an organization is more inclined to the "ego" side, emphasis is on management and bureaucracy. Environmental constraints and dangers take priority, and the organization starts focusing on reacting accordingly, analyzing situations correctly and following the appropriate plans and strategies. Permission is required before any action can be taken and team members must maintain their prescribed roles.

When an organization is more inclined to the "soul" side, emphasis is on leadership and entrepreneurial activities. The environmental focus is on opportunities, and proactive risk-taking is encouraged. Energy and emotional intelligence are as much a part of guiding the decision making process as strategy. Values related to customer-focused vision and mission determine priorities, which inspire and drive action.

In both individuals and organizations, it is important to keep a balance between the two dimensions. The bigger the vision is, the more ambition is needed in order to reach achieve it. Similarly, the bigger the ambition is, the more important it is to expand the vision. Ego without soul creates "blind ambition." Soul without ego can lead to impotence and or "burnout."

1.13 The Three Core SFM Models

There are three core models that have been developed using the Success Factor Modeling methodology that are applied as part of generative consulting: The SFM Circle of Success, the SFM Leadership Model and the SFM Collective Intelligence Model. These models, and their associated skills and tools, are described in Robert Dilts' three-volume book series on Success Factor Modeling.

The *SFM Circle of Success* is about developing an entrepreneurial mindset. It focuses on the outcomes of personal satisfaction, financial robustness and profitability, scalable growth, innovation and resilience. To achieve these outcomes, you need to actively engage your customers, your team members, your partners, your stakeholders and your investors. Developing a Circle of Success is especially useful for companies and organizations who are in a phase of growth, as we will see in Chapter 2.

The *SFM Leadership Model* focuses on the organizational outcomes necessary to build and sustain a Circle of Success, especially through in times of challenge and change. These outcomes involve promoting change, achieving results, developing people, and realizing values. These outcomes are achieved through the leadership actions of empowering, coaching, sharing and stretching. The SFM Leadership Model is valuable for many situations, but it is especially important for companies in order to survive a crisis, as is described in Chapter 3.

The *SFM Collective Intelligence Model* maps out the skills and conditions necessary to improve collaboration in order to generate new ideas, find creative solutions, increase or enhance performance and make wise decisions. These outcomes are supported through the actions of collective benchmarking, sharing best practices, brainstorming and generative collaboration. The SFM Collective Intelligence Model is particularly useful for groups and organizations that are in transition, as we will show in Chapter 4.

Many situations will require a combination of these models and the skills and tools that they provide. A consultant will very often help an organization to align a number of different outcomes. To make a meaningful contribution, for instance, an organization will have to develop its people and make wise decisions. Achieving profitability and financial stability will often need to be aligned with enhancing performance and achieving results, and so on.

Obviously, determining where an intervention needs to focus within an organization, and what issues need to be addressed, is the essence of all successful consulting work. As we pointed out earlier, when working with situations that are completely new and unprecedented, it is not possible to use "off- the- shelf" solutions that have worked in the past. Consultants and their client organizations must have a fundamental problem-solving structure that allows them to identify their key issues and the resources needed for change. A good example of how to put all of the pieces together is presented in Chapter 5.

1.14 The S.C.O.R.E. Model

The basic format for gathering information in generative consulting is what is known as the S.C.O.R.E. Model. This model was developed by Robert Dilts and Todd Epstein (co-founder with Dilts of NLP University in Santa Cruz, California) in 1987 to describe the process that they were intuitively using to define problems and to design interventions.

The letters "S.C.O.R.E." stand for **S**ymptoms, **C**auses, **O**utcomes, **R**esources and **E**ffects. According to the model, these represent the minimum number of elements that need to be addressed by any process of change. The S.C.O.R.E. Model indicates that effective problem-solving ability involves defining the "problem space" and identifying potential areas of "solution space" by establishing the relationship between the following elements:

1. **Symptoms** are typically the most noticeable and conspicuous elements of a present problem or problem state.
2. **Causes** are the underlying elements responsible for creating and maintaining the symptoms. They are usually less obvious than the symptoms that they produce.
3. **Outcomes** are the desired states or results that will take the place of the symptoms.
4. **Resources** are the elements (skills, tools, beliefs, etc.) which can be used to transform the causes of the symptoms and achieve and maintain desired outcomes.
5. **Effects** are the longer-term results of achieving a particular outcome. Specific outcomes are generally stepping stones to produce a longer- term effect.
   a. Positive effects are often the reason or motivation for establishing a particular outcome.
   b. Negative effects can produce resistance or ecological problems.

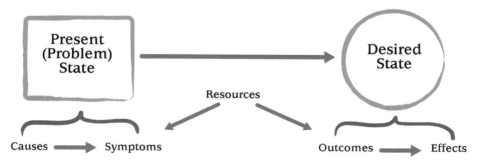

The S.C.O.R.E. Model defines the basic elements to be addressed by any process of change

To better understand the S.C.O.R.E. distinctions, consider the following questions: *What is a problem? What makes something a problem? What important elements define a problem and help to successfully resolve it?*

Outcomes

First, it is important to realize that if you have no *outcome*, you have no problem. If you do not want to be anywhere else than where you are, you have no problem. In fact, the process of establishing a goal often creates a problem. A "problem" is the difference between your present state and your desired state, and it involves issues to address in order to achieve the desired state.

It is also important to realize that if you have no outcome in mind, you have no possibility of a solution, because you do not know where you are trying to go. Thus, defining outcomes is perhaps the most essential part of problem-solving. Where are you trying to go? What needs to be different?

Remember that, in generative change, the outcome is something new, unprecedented and difficult to define in specific terms. It is stated and represented as an intention or direction of change, as opposed to a clearly defined destination. Another important consideration relates to what level, or combination of levels, of change the outcome is focused: environment, behavior, capabilities, values and beliefs, identity or purpose. This will determine a lot about what types of challenges will be involved and the types of resources that will be needed.

The types of questions that a generative consultant would use to explore organizational outcomes with a client include: *What do you most want to create for your clients? Your team? Your stakeholders? Your partners? Your company? What do you want more of? What do you want less of? What is the next level to which you want to move?*

Symptoms

In the process of moving toward a desired state, *symptoms* come up in the form of constraints, resistances and interferences to progress toward or achieving the outcome. Symptoms are typically the most obvious aspects of a problem and generally the reason why organizations reach out to consultants. In organizations, symptoms may take the form of quality issues, loss of profitability, slow growth, lack of innovation, employee absenteeism, customer complaints, and so on.

Thus, typical types of symptoms in an organization might be a drop in profit, motivation, innovation or productivity. In teams, behavioral symptoms may show up as a lack of energy, initiative or agility. Symptoms related to mindset occur in the form of lack of motivation, stress, inner conflict or emotional struggle.

The way in which we define, understand and deal with symptoms is a key part of generative consulting. The concepts of *complementarity* and *compensation* are key principles of generative consulting. These are essentially an extension of the notion in physics that "for every action there is an equal and opposite reaction." If you breathe in, you will eventually have to breathe out. If you exert a lot of energy, you will eventually have to rest.

The principle of complementarity maintains that whenever you try to move or expand in a particular direction, you will engage all of the balancing forces. For instance, as soon as an organization announces: "We are going to increase our profits by fifteen percent," guess what will happen? All the opposing forces will immediately begin to show up, such as production or quality problems or issues related to the motivation, innovation or effort needed to achieve that desired outcome. When we are unaware of this dynamic of compensation, attempts at solutions can actually make things worse.

Effective generative consultants need to be aware that some form of compensation will happen and that addressing it will be a key part of the work. If you do not expect it, it will come as an unpleasant surprise. If you treat it as an enemy, it is going to become an escalating problem. Being able to develop a generative state is essential for working with such natural complementarities and compensations and finding creative ways to maintain balance.

As we pointed out earlier, many symptoms emerge when we neglect to take into account key parts of the holarchy in which we are operating. Viewed from this perspective, symptoms are not merely problems to discard. Instead, they are a communication that some important part of the holon is being overlooked or ignored. In that sense, the symptom is actually an important contribution to finding the solutions.

According to the principle of complementarity, symptoms generally emerge as a type of mirror image to of the outcome (and vice versa). That is, if the outcome is to create an increase in profitability, symptoms will necessarily show up as areas of decline in revenue. If the outcome is to "innovate," symptoms will come in the form of old habits and resistance to change. Symptoms also tend to mirror the level(s) of change related to the outcome: environment, behavior, capabilities, values and beliefs, identity or purpose.

* If the outcome is to extend a market (environment), symptoms will show up as a limited or shrinking market.

* If the outcome is to innovate (behavior), symptoms will show up as repetition of or regression to old habits.

* If the outcome is to increase production capacity (capability), symptoms will show up as blockages to or reductions of that capacity.

* If the outcome is to promote the importance of customer service (values and beliefs), symptoms will show up as precedence taken by other things or distraction by other priorities.

* If the outcome is to step into an expanded role in a particular industry (identity), symptoms will show up as inertia in or nostalgia for the previous identity.

* If the outcome is to transform people's lives through new technologies (purpose), symptoms will would show up as the ways in which those technologies might be damaging to the organization's customers.

Very often, the conflicts that emerge between symptoms and outcomes are an expression of the dynamic balance between ego and soul.

Symptoms may be identified and explored by asking questions, such as: *What is the problem? What isn't working as it should for your clients? Your team? Your stakeholders? Your partners? Your organization? What is the situation you need to change? What is going wrong or giving you trouble? What is stopping the team/group/organization from moving in the right direction?*

Causes

Of course, effective problem-solving involves finding and resolving the deeper *causes* of a particular symptom or set of symptoms. What you identify as the cause determines where you will seek to create the solution.

Treating the symptom alone will only bring temporary relief. Causes are often less obvious, broader and more systemic in nature than the particular symptoms they are producing. A drop in profit or productivity may be the result of issues relating to competition, organization, leadership, market changes, technology changes or communication channels.

Causes often involve a different level of factors than the symptoms they produce. For instance, symptoms showing up at the level of environment would most likely be caused by inappropriate actions. Problems at the level of behavior could be caused by missing or inappropriate capabilities. Problems or confusions at a capability level are likely to be related to unclear or conflicting values or beliefs. Conflicts of values may relate to confusion at an identity level. Identity struggles can be caused by the lack of a clear or compelling purpose.

Another important area of "cause" for a particular symptom relates to the potentially positive purposes or *secondary gains* provided by the symptom. For instance, a drop in profit, innovation or productivity may be related to the secondary gain of avoiding stress and failure. This important area of potential causes is often overlooked. When working with organizations, identifying the "secondary gain" related to a particular problem or symptom is often crucial. People can actually draw benefits from issues like confusion, chaos and inefficiency.

In companies and organizations, symptoms are also often created by the lack of alignment between different parts of the holarchy, such as – i.e., teams, functions, divisions, business units, executive board, etc. Looking for areas of misalignment is thus an important part of a generative consultant's job.

Misalignment can also be the result of differences in *lines of development*. Not all parts of an organizational holarchy have the same degree of development. Not everybody on a team has the same competences or levels of competency in every area. One of the main mistakes in consulting is to presume that everyone in an organization has the same degree of ability and understanding.

In summary, causes may be explored and discovered by asking questions, such as: *Where is the symptom coming from? What is triggering or creating the symptom? What was going on just before, or at the time when the symptom started? What is holding the symptom in place? What prevents you from changing the symptom? What is the positive intention behind the symptom – what purpose does it serve? Are there any positive consequences that result or have resulted from this symptom?*

Effects

Defining the longer-term desired *effects* of achieving a particular goal or outcome is a significant factor in creating a sustainable solution. Some important important questions to explore include "What are you trying to achieve with that outcome? Where does that outcome lead to in the longer-term?" A particular outcome is generally one step along a path to longer-range effects. It is important for the solution to a problem to be congruent with the organization's longer-term desired effects or broader vision and ambitions.

A major problem with many organizations is an overly short-term focus. They are too myopic. Sometimes the way in which an outcome is achieved can actually interfere with reaching the longer-term target; i.e. it is possible to "win the battle, but lose the war."

The short-term focus is a natural consequence of what we have called the CRASH state. This is one of the reasons why the COACH state and generative state are so important.

Similar to the relationship between causes and symptoms, effects are often at a different level of change than outcomes and usually relate to a hierarchically deeper level. For instance, outcomes at the level of environment are frequently intended to support the possibility of new behavior. Outcomes at the level of behavior support the development of new capabilities. New capabilities are often developed to support particular organizational values or beliefs. In turn, strengthening values and beliefs support growth at an identity level. Identity development serves a larger or more expanded purpose.

Questions related to effects include: *What would happen if you achieved your outcome? What will it do for you to attain your goal? What benefits would there be for your clients? Your team? Your stakeholders? Your partners? Your company? After achieving your outcome, what will you do or what will happen next? What is the longer-term vision and ambition?*

Resources

In order to find the resources that will produce an effective solution for a particular business situation, it is necessary to know the symptoms and their causes as well as the outcome and the ultimate desired effect to be reached. Sometimes the resources needed to address the problem state are different from those necessary to achieve the outcome. Other times, a single resource will effectively address the entire situation. It is useful, however, to explore both resources that would help to (a) address the symptom and its causes and (b) achieve the desired outcome and effects.

The required resources will depend on the level of factors, or combination of levels, that are involved in the situation to be addressed: environment, behavior, capabilities, values and beliefs, identity or purpose. As Albert Einstein once pointed out, *we cannot solve a problem with the same level of thinking that is creating the problem.* In general, resources need to be found at a deeper, more foundational level than the problem itself. However, multiple levels of resources will frequently need to be engaged to produce an effective, generative solution.

Identifying resources involves asking questions, such as: *What* (behavior, state, ability, belief, support, etc.) *is necessary to achieve the outcome* (solve the problem)*? Have you ever achieved an outcome* (or solved a problem) *like this before? What did you do? Do you know if an outcome* (or problem) *like this has ever been achieved* (or solved) *before by other individuals/teams/organizations? What did they do? If you and your clients had already achieved the outcome* (solved the problem), *and were looking back at how you had done it, what would be the key resources needed? What other choices exist that could maintain the positive intent or consequences of the problem while still allowing the individuals/teams/organizations to achieve the desired state?*

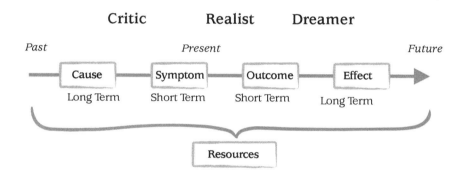

1.15 Applying the S.C.O.R.E. Model

One effective way to conceptualize and use the S.C.O.R.E. Model distinctions is to organize these elements along a time line. Typically, symptoms are experienced by a client in the present or in the recent past. The causes of such symptoms tend to precede them in time. That is, the cause of a symptom comes before it in time, either immediately before or potentially much earlier.

Outcomes occur in the future with respect to symptoms. They are the desired results that will take the place of the symptoms. Effects are the longer-term results of achieving particular outcomes. Resources can come from anywhere in time.

In conclusion, in generative consulting work, we apply the S.C.O.R.E. framework in order to define an organization's challenge and identify a potential solution. Examples of how the S.C.O.R.E. framework can be applied to map out potential challenges and solutions will be provided in the following chapters.

To be generative, we cannot apply the S.C.O.R.E. framework by simply considering words and numbers. Generative consulting brings together multiple intelligences. We encourage clients to represent each element of the S.C.O.R.E. somatically, visually and metaphorically, in addition to verbally. And for effective generative change, we need to work with the three connections necessary to create and sustain a generative state: (1) a somatic center in the body, (2) an intention or direction for the future and (3) the field of resources necessary to bring that intention or direction into a concrete expression.

1.16 Generative Consulting Road Map

Generative consulting work involves always targeting the longer-term effects of the intervention toward creating greater resilience, sustainability and ecological, win-win results for the largest possible amount of the holarchy.

Organizational Ecosystems

Applying the concepts of holon and holarchy to the consulting process, we can view an organization as part of a larger ecosystem that includes the state of the economy, the evolution of the market and its relation to its own organizational life-cycle.

The State of the Economy – The economy can be expanding, stable or receding. This will clearly create opportunities or constraints to which an organization will need to respond.

The Phase of Market Evolution – An organization may be in an emerging market, a developing market or a mature market. This will create important conditions that will necessarily influence the organization's decisions and actions.

The Organizational Life-Cycle – Another key factor is the life-cycle of the venture. Organizations themselves go through different phases of a life-cycle. They start up from an initial idea or vision, they grow, they become stable and then they usually reach a point of either renewal or decline.

The types of situations where generative consulting is most relevant and needed are settings where the dynamics making up an organization's ecosystem intersect to create conditions that nobody has ever had to deal with before – circumstances that demand a completely new response.

For instance, an organization may have to find a way to renew itself or its product line that is completely different than anything it has done before. The change might even have to be entirely different from anything done in the organization's market before. Apple's ability to renew itself through new products like the iPod, iPhone, iPad and Apple Watch is a good example of that.

Organizational Impact and Responses to Changes in the Ecosystem

Depending on the intersection of these different stages in its ecosystem, an organization may be in a state of:

Stimulating Growth –Needing to increase output capacity, revenues, sales and size, etc. Generativity is generally necessary for growth, especially if the organization is venturing into a new area,; such as trying to grow into an emerging market that has not previously existed. During a *growth* phase an organization will need to put an emphasis on developing an entrepreneurial mindset and strengthening or expanding their Circle of Success. (See Chapter 2.)

Surviving Crisis –Needing to reduce waste and expenses, reengineer processes, recover sales/customers, etc. In many crisis situations, the old ways no longer work. What used to be effective no longer produces successful results and may even make things worse. So, it becomes necessary to create a whole new way of doing things. During a time of *crisis*, an organization will need to put emphasis be on developing and strengthening *leadership* and *resilience*. (See Chapter 3).

Managing Transition – Needing to prepare for inner or outer changes by optimizing structures and processes, etc. Adapting to change requires transition, especially to avoid crisis. An organization may not be trying to grow or be experiencing a crisis, but still needs to adapt to changes in its ecosystem. It may be doing its best to survive and thrive, but everything else is changing. So, it must creatively adapt by doing things that are unfamiliar or unprecedented. During a period of *transition*, the organization will need to put emphasis on fostering and harnessing *collective intelligence*. (See Chapter 4.)

Naturally, these three types of situations and responses are not completely separate from one another. Sometimes growth leads to crisis. An organization may be growing and, as long as it stays within a certain boundaries, everything is fine. But if it starts growing too fast, it does not have the necessary structure in place, or has insufficient financing or other resources, and it ends up in crisis.

Tesla Motors ran into that problem with their Model 3. They were unable to keep up with all the orders for this car and, as a result, the company went into a major crisis. It was reported that CEO Elon Musk was spending 120 hours a week at the office and was eating poorly. Too much success in one area can create major trouble in other parts of the holon.

A generative consultant understands that it is not possible to control all of these outer forces. Those ecosystem dynamics create situations that need to be creatively dealt with. To respond effectively to these outer dynamics, it is necessary to examine the inner structure and capabilities of the venture and consider: "Is the company and all of its parts sufficiently resilient? Is it prepared to respond appropriately and effectively? Is it taking the proper actions to prepare for the future?"

The answers to these questions have to do with an organization's capacity for entrepreneurship, leadership and collective intelligence. How these three capabilities are mobilized and combined determines how effectively and creatively an organization, a venture or a team will respond to its external circumstances. Even for an organization of only one member, there will still be a need for self-leadership. And it is still possible for single individual to mobilize collective intelligence by reaching out to advisors, partners and other supporters.

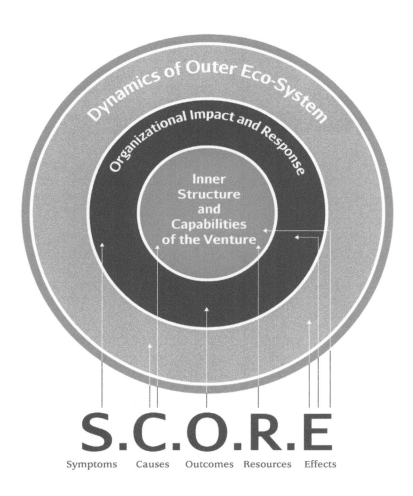

Outer ecosystem dynamics and their impact on the inner structure and capabilities of a venture determine its response.

In summary, **Outcomes** and **Symptoms** relate to the *organizational impact* and demands of dynamics imposed by the *outer ecosystem* (economy, stage of market evolution, organizational life-cycle) and the ensuing *inner response* from the venture (i.e. stimulating growth, surviving crisis, managing transition).

Causes and **Resources** will come from both *outer ecosystem* dynamics and the *inner structure and capabilities* of the venture (i.e. the condition of its "Circle of Success, mindset, leadership, level of collective intelligence, etc.).

The different SFM models can be applied to support the response of an organization to changes in its outer ecosystem.

1.17 The SFM DIAMOND Model

The Seven Steps of Generative Consulting

There are seven steps and nine core competences that characterize generative consulting. There are many, many ways to do each step, but what is common to all those steps are the competences that are needed to do them appropriately and properly.

The first step is to gather information and *diagnose the key conditions of an organization's present state.* Is it in a state of growth, crisis or transition; or some combination of them? What dynamics are taking place in its ecosystem and in the other parts of the organizational holarchy? This is a crucial stage. To do it well, a generative consultant might have to gather information from a whole group of people, sometimes dozens or even hundreds of people.

Step two is to establish the desired state and *intended direction of change.* This will determine the amount of generativity required by the organization and its constituents. It involves defining what has to change, as well as when, where and how much.

The third step is to do *action planning*, potentially integrating multiple levels of change. This is often accomplished through the process of developing a story-board defining the course of actions key members of the organization will need to take.

Step four is to implement the plan by *moving into action* engaging all of the relevant actors in the organization. Effective action requires both knowledge and energy – knowing what to do and being motivated to do it.

This naturally leads to the fifth step, which involves identifying and addressing the *obstacles, challenges and interferences* that will inevitably arise. Obstacles will sometimes show up very actively and prominently while other times obstacles will come in the form of "passive resistance."

The **sixth step** of the generative consulting methodology is to determine and *note the progress of the change.* Key to any change process is the ability to assess progress and make necessary adjustments. This frequently requires collective benchmarking. Tracking the progress of a new change process cannot be accomplished by rigidly applying former key performance indicators or outdated measures of success. For instance, the tracking process may need to focus on the rate of change – not necessarily how much has happened in a particular period, but instead how quickly something is changing.

Step seven is to help put into place practices that allow the organization to sustain and *deepen the change* that has taken place. Practice is particularly significant – if anything is to be changed, key stakeholders have to be involved in ongoing practice. The members of the relevant organizational holarchy parts need to constantly practice learning new habits; especially those relating to mindset.

As a way to help remember and apply these seven steps, we have developed what we refer to as the **SFM DIAMOND Model**™ (special thanks to Jean-François Thiriet for suggesting the acronym).

At the core of the SFM DIAMOND Model are the seven steps of generative consulting that form the acronym DIAMOND. The following table summarizes the seven fundamental facets of the DIAMOND Model and the icons we have chosen to symbolize them: a stethoscope for Defining the present state; a navigational compass for Intention setting; a map for

Action planning; a rocket ship for Moving into action; a traffic barrier for Obstacle transforming; a set of measuring calipers for Noting progress and a meditating Buddha for Deepening practices:

Defining Present State: Gathering information and diagnosing the current situation.

Intention Setting: Establishing the desired state / direction for change.

Action Planning: Building a critical path.

Moving to Action: Executing the plan.

Obstacle Transforming: Dealing with challenges and pitfalls.

Noting Progress: Assessing and measuring change.

Deepening Practices: Follow up for sustaining and deepening the changes.

The SFM DIAMOND Model represents these steps as the facets of a diamond rather than a simple linear series of actions. One important implication of the metaphor of a diamond is that the steps are not necessarily always done in a linear manner. For a process to be both comprehensive and generative, we may need to return to some steps multiple times or conduct certain steps in parallel. Working as a generative consultant, you may, at times, be applying different steps to different parts of the organizational system (or holon).

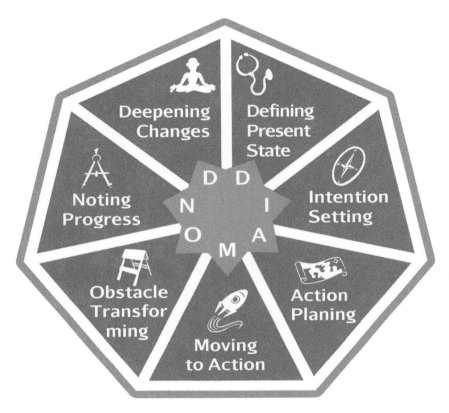

The Core of the SFM DIAMOND Model is Formed by
the Seven Steps of Generative Consulting

The Nine Competences of Generative Consulting

Key to applying these seven steps in the Generative Consulting DIAMOND Model is the ability to establish and maintain a generative state of "creative flow", in both consultants and their clients. This state emerges from the interplay of cognitive, somatic and relational dynamics. In order to accomplish this you will need to develop and strengthen the *Nine Core Competences of Generative Consulting*:

Systemic thinking – the ability to see how elements fit into the bigger picture and work with multiple perspectives / truths. This is essential in order to make sure that the key elements of the organizational holarchy have been considered and addressed. It is particularly important for gathering information and action planning.

Influencing skills – the ability to persuade through presence, congruence and alignment. An effective consultant needs to motivate and influence key people to take action, especially when those actions are unfamiliar and potentially risky.

Emotional intelligence – the ability to work with emotional states and detect emotional undercurrents (e.g., the shadow/"elephant in the room" no one is talking about). This is an essential competence for identifying and addressing obstacles and resistance.

Facilitation skills – the ability to recognize and support resonance and synergy between members of a group. This competence is potentially important for each step of the generative consulting process, in order to obtain high-quality input from all of the relevant actors and stakeholders.

Communication skills – fluency in talking to different types and levels of people. This is another essential area of competence for all the steps of generative consulting. A consultant's effectiveness and livelihood is based on his or her ability to communicate effectively to a variety of people.

Presentation skills – the ability to address an audience using multiple communication channels (verbal, visual, metaphorical, somatic, etc.). A consultant's success ultimately depends upon his or her ability to present information and proposals for action and change.

Relational skills – the ability to establish rapport and create trust. An effective consultant needs to establish trusting relationships with clients for there to be meaningful change. Without trust, people are unwilling to try something new and take risks.

Pattern detection skills – the ability to identify different levels of trends and meaning in sets of data and interpersonal interactions by tuning into both strong and weak signals. A good consultant needs to detect patterns on several levels and in different parts of a holarchy.

Strategic thinking – the ability to work on both ambition and vision (meaning and purpose) and see how smaller steps create a critical path to a larger outcome. This is clearly one of the most important competences for effective action planning.

The following table summarizes the nine generative consulting competences and the icons we have chosen to symbolize them.

 Systemic thinking: Seeing how things fit into the bigger picture and working with multiple perspectives / truths.

 Influencing skills: Persuading through presence, congruence and alignment.

 Emotional intelligence: Working with emotional states and detecting the emotional undercurrents in a given situation (e.g., the shadow/elephant in the room no one is talking about).

 Facilitation skills: Recognizing and supporting resonance and synergy between members of a group.

 Communication skills: Transmitting key information to different types and levels of people (hierarchy, education, culture).

 Presentation skills: Speaking to an audience using multiple communication channels (verbal, visual, metaphorical, somatic, etc).

 Relational skills: Establishing rapport and creating trust.

 Pattern detection skills: Spotting different levels of trends and meaning in sets of data and interpersonal interactions by tuning into both strong and weak signals.

 Strategic thinking: Working on both ambition and vision (meaning and purpose) and seeing how smaller steps create a critical path to a larger outcome.

[Note: For detailed score cards on all the 9 competencies please see Appendix I]

In the SFM DIAMOND Model, we represent the nine generative consulting competences as another layer of facets surrounding the seven steps of generative consulting. We have positioned the competences closest to the steps for which they are most helpful and relevant:

The Relationship of Key Generative Consulting Competences to the Seven Steps of the SFM DIAMOND Model

Organizational Challenges Requiring Generative Change

The final layer of facets of the SFM DIAMOND Model represents the three fundamental organizational challenges requiring generative change:

1. Stimulating Growth

2. Surviving Crisis

3. Managing Transition

Clearly, all of the nine generative consulting competences are relevant to each stage of change. However, some of these competences are more critical to some stages and challenges than others, as we will see in the next chapters. We can represent these relationships in the following diagram:

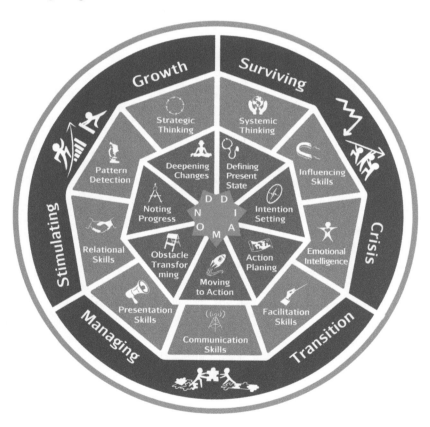

The SFM DIAMOND Model of Generative Consulting

In Chapters 2 to 4, we will show how to apply the generative consulting principles and the S.C.O.R.E. Model along with the seven steps and nine competences, in order to address the key issues of stimulating growth, surviving crisis and managing transition. We will provide further clarification and case examples for each challenge and how the generative consulting steps and competences can be applied to produce creative and sustainable results.

Organizations may also experience any combination of these stages, depending on their life-cycle and the state of their larger ecosystem. In Chapter 5, we will illustrate how generative consulting can be applied to help organizations that have a complex mix of challenges.

In our concluding Chapter 6, we bring together all contributing authors to share with you how, on a personal level, the implementation of the generative consulting approach has made a difference in our work and our lives, how it shapes our creativity and innovation as well as that of our clients.

We are excited and honored to have you join us on this journey.

"The world as we have created it is a process of our thinking. It cannot be changed without changing our thinking."

— Albert Einsten

"Some people dream of success, while other people get up every morning and make it happen."

— Wayne Huizenga

Chapter 2
Managing Growth
in Business

Colette Normandeau and Robert B. Dilts

2.1 Overview

In this chapter, we focus on how, as generative consultants and generative business leaders, you can best support and ignite a business' growth through a generative approach. You will learn how a venture can achieve a balance between ego and soul by applying the SFM Circle of Success™ Model and the SFM Success Mindset Map™. As mentioned in chapter one, the key areas addressed in the SFM Circle of Success™ will help a business with profitability, scalable growth, meaningful contribution, and innovation and resilience. This chapter also provides an in-depth look at how optimal mindsets form the foundation upon which to succeed and flourish. The various exercises and tools proposed will help improve your competences as a leader of change.

2.2 Why is this chapter important?

Imagine building a castle on toothpicks! What will happen at the first gust of wind?

The elements covered in this chapter are necessary foundations upon which any business can be built. Sustainable growth is possible when foundations are set on solid ground. If you are missing a pillar or a wall or if the earth below is uneven, your castle will crumble down. When your foundations are strong, possibilities are endless and generative success is attainable. You, as a generative consultant or generative business leader, will be the locksmith, and the SFM models will be the keys. They will unlock the true potential of a venture and set the course for yours or your client's business to rise high and shine. Through a better understanding and experience of the skills of generative consulting, you will hone your craft and help yourself and your clients take your ventures to new levels of success.

2.3 What is growth? - Setting the context

Growth is both a noun and an adjective. It depicts an act, a process, a stage in development, an increase in value over a certain period or the expansion of a business. The Old English root word is *growan*, "to grow or flourish."

In times of growth, businesses strive to generate the means to sustainably increase their customer base, their revenues, their output capacity, the number of their team members, and so on. During a growth phase, the venture's emphasis will be on developing an entrepreneurial mindset and strengthening, or expanding, what we refer to in Success Factor Modeling (SFM) as their *Circle of Success* (CoS). The ability to grow effectively also requires agility and a high degree of innovation. Therefore, growth is a classic situation calling for generative change, especially if the venture is a start-up or is trying to grow into an emerging market that has not previously existed.

Before delving into the SFM Circle of Success model, let's look at the current context and circumstances of ventures and start-ups.

Importance of the growth phase for a business

Back in 2001 in my early years as an entrepreneur, statistics stated that only two out five businesses survived the two-year mark. According to *Forbes Magazine*, the numbers for 2018 were quite similar: half survived five years and one in three survived the ten-year mark[1]. Disconnection to market needs, poor business savvy, lack of funds to maintain business or attract investors and inability to create or support a high-level functioning team are among the main causes of business failure. As mentioned in Chapter 1, *mindset* produces *actions*, which, in turn, create *outcomes*. Gloomy statistics showing low success rates tend to hinder an entrepreneurial growth mindset. Thoughts and doubts like: "Is this going to work?", "Will I be one of those who do or don't make it?", "Am I cut out to be a successful entrepreneur?" or "Do I have what it takes?" keep lingering in mind, as they did in mine during the first two years after launching my business.

During my own start-up phase, I had to create a business plan to obtain the funds to support my new venture. I found that producing such a plan was an even more painful delivery than birthing my two kids.

---

[1]   https://www.forbes.com/sites/forbesfinancecouncil/2018/10/25/what-per-centage-of-small-businesses-fail-and-how-can-you-avoid-being-one-of-them/#2722e18643b5

https://smallbiztrends.com/2019/03/startup-statistics-small-business.html

I remember thinking: "Do I really need this?" "Am I actually going to use this?" The good news is that the knowledge I acquired by doing the business plan provided a solid base to make my business sustainable... although that is not what kept me going. What helped through my start-up years and growth periods were actually thoughts and entrepreneurial mindsets aligned with what Robert Dilts and his late brother John Dilts created and called the "SFM Circle of Success" (CoS).

Whether in the start-up or scale-up phase of its life cycle, a venture naturally requires the capacity to grow. However, a company's potential for growth is continuously affected by economic fluctuations, emerging technologies and ever-changing markets. This makes a venture's growth phase paramount! It determines whether the venture will make it in the marketplace or not. The capacity of a venture for growth lies in establishing a solid foundation, which allows it to manage the inevitable crises and transitions successfully. As described in the following chapters, as a generative consultant and business leader, you will most definitely be an invaluable ally in enabling a venture's success and prosperity during these phases.

Growth is not just about surviving... it's about thriving.

2.4 Growth issues and challenges

Major challenges can occur when ventures are striving to grow in a receding economy or a mature market. Challenges may involve increased competition or insufficient essential resources to grow (finance, people, technical resources, etc.).

Ventures that lack the knowledge, the collaborative ability and the necessary leadership to create a scalable structure, as outlined by the SFM Circle of Success, will struggle to grow, even in a favorable ecosystem. This can undermine motivation and ambition and result in too much or not enough "Dreamer."

Defining Present State

Whether a challenge is internally or externally created, a first good step to properly support a venture is gathering information and detecting present issues and concerns. We refer here to the **first step** of the seven-steps of generative consulting in the SFM DIAMOND model: **Defining the Present State**. This step involves *gathering information and diagnosing the current situation* in order to identify the growth challenges facing the venture.

Pattern Detection

Relational Skills

As a skillful generative consultant and business leader, you will need to use several of the key generative consulting competences. For instance, *Relational Skills* and *Pattern Detection Skills* are necessary to determine a venture's present state (symptoms and causes) and desired state (outcomes and effects), in order to lay the path to close the gap between those two states by identifying the key elements upon which to focus.

Vital elements to investigate while stimulating growth

The S.C.O.R.E. model, which was presented in depth in Chapter 1, can best support the first and second steps of the SFM Generative Consulting DIAMOND Model. It addresses five core elements of any situation and provides an overview of the full spectrum of a venture's system. Using the S.C.O.R.E. model will also support a shift in thinking from problems to solutions and improve the correlation between outcomes and proposed actions and resources.

Let's use the S.C.O.R.E. Model to explore common issues and desires that come up during a venture's growth phase.

Note: For this presentation, we will use only the first four components of the model, thus excluding effects.

Stimulating Growth

Symptoms	Possible Causes — Outer	Possible Causes — Inner	Desired Outcomes	Possible Resources
• Slow market response • Resistance, stuck state, inertia • No more drive to move forward • Leaders/business owners experiencing a false start or not knowing how to start	• Stable or receding economy • Increasing competition, lack of resources (financial, people, etc.) • Start-up, Scale-up or renewal phase of life-cycle	• Inadequate structure to scale up ineffective team • Low motivation/ ambition • Too much or not enough "Dreamer" • Challenges offset the venture's plans and motivation • Team members have lost sight of their passion and purpose • Lack of perseverance	• Enthusiastic • Motivated • Connected to what fuels leaders/ business owners and team members • Agility and creativity and major innovations to work through challenges • Increased output capacity, sales, revenues and size	• Growth mindset • Explore passions • Create a compelling vision • Develop a balanced Circle of Success • Collaboration Spiral (see Chapter 4 on transitions)
• Difficulty attracting and retaining customers	• Many offers on the market, less distinction	• Lack of inspiring vision and clear ambition • Market segment or ideal client not clearly or adequately defined	• Attract 20 new clients within the next two years and retain them • Build client satisfaction and trust with a clear process	• Develop a balanced Circle of Success • Clear Vision • Establish ambitions • Awaken generativity to determine uniqueness • Hire a customer service representative.

- Business announces that "Our vision is to be the reference in the field of…"
- Great soul-based vision, but not ambitious enough goals or concrete actions to attain them

- Influenced by other companies' presentations
- Copy-paste

- Confusion between what is vision and ambition
- Imbalance between soul and ego

- Clear goals
- Inspiring client-based vision
- Confidence
- Audacity
- Aligned actions

- Application of CoS model
- Review of beliefs and growth mindset

- No mobilization and team members having a hard time following the leader or stuck in a day-to-day grind
- Confusion in system
- Things not being done, running in circles
- Actions not creating the best possible outcomes, energy spread thin, lack of focus

- Comparison with other workplaces
- Dealing on a daily basis with market and customer emergencies

- Different generations
- Too many directions
- Leaders know where there are going, but the information is not communicated to teams
- Teams and members are not clear on their roles
- Entrepreneurs try to be good in everything – 'jack of all trades', but then become 'master of none'

- Big picture clarity
- Communicate with charisma
- Mobilized team
- Alignment with VMAR (Vision Mission, Ambition, Role)
- High-functioning teams and better generative collaboration
- Harmony, balance, focus

- Create compelling future
- Communicate with multiple intelligences
- Develop emotional intelligence – Mindset compass / COACH state
- Define "superpowers"

How about you? What are your present client's situations? Take time to reflect on your client's present situation and desired outcomes. You may also want to reflect on your own business as a generative consultant and business leader.

Symptoms	Causes	Outcomes	Resources

Personally, I like to remind myself when things get tough and issues arise that "I just haven't found the best possible way to achieve my desired outcomes yet." This mindset derives from William Ross Ashby's *law of requisite variety*[2]. It stipulates that for a system to be stable, the number of states that its control mechanism can attain (its variety) must be greater than or equal to the number of states in the system being controlled. This means that, in a system, the element with the most flexibility is the one that survives and is more likely to thrive. As a generative consultant and business leader, your role is to awaken this type of thinking in order to best support the success of a venture confronted with challenging issues.

All (business) issues whether caused by outer or inner circumstances are opportunities to spark creativity and foster innovation. "Innovate or die" has been a business mantra for a while! If we take a quick stroll down memory lane, in the early 1900's, it could take 50 to 60 years for a business to renew. Now with technological advancements and present ecosystems, there is pressure on businesses to change rapidly, be even more flexible and innovative, and review and renew their business strategies anywhere from every three months to every two years.

If necessity is the mother of innovation...
...generativity can be its father.[3]

Many ventures have embarked on the journey of disruptive innovation – disrupt or be disrupted to find solutions. For some, it has been costly because these changes did not always align with the business' core purpose or connect to its market needs. Many disruptive innovations are created out of fear and not passion and purpose. Our times are calling for generative solutions and generative change. Through the SFM DIAMOND Model, we wish to support you as a consultant and leader of change to become even more generative and nourish ecological generativity in ventures.

For every problem there is a generative solution, whether entrepreneurs/leaders know it or not! Your role is to spark that generativity in your client and/or your team.

---

2   Robert Dilts - *Law of Requisite Variety* (1998) NLP University Press

3   Original quote- "Necessity is the mother of invention." Plato

2.5 Supporting growth with a generative approach

As a generative consultant, helping entrepreneurs and conscious leaders of all types to build an effective, balanced and scalable *Circle of Success* will be a major mission for you. Whether a venture wants to increase its output capacity, revenues, sales and size, or foster agility and major innovations, each of these outcomes are addressed in this model. This makes it a powerful tool to help you detect which key factors a venture needs to address on in order to achieve its desired outcomes.

To support sustainable growth in a venture, you will also want to develop a positive entrepreneurial mindset – a growth mindset – whether it be yours, as the internal change leader or your client's. To grow effectively and sustainably, it is paramount for ventures to have "big-picture" clarity and a compelling vision of the future they are trying to create, establish habits of success and be clear about their ongoing priorities.

Key mindsets for growth

A successful growth mindset is comprised of three levels:

      1. Meta Mindset – Big-picture clarity

      2. Macro Mindset – Habits of success

      3. Micro Mindset – Ongoing priorities

Meta Mindset has to do with our fundamental attitude toward our work, the world and our place in that world. It relates to success factors at the levels of *purpose* and *identity*. Meta Mindset is essentially made up of a sense of passion, vision, mission, ambition and role. These key elements defined help provide *"big-picture clarity"* within a venture.

Macro Mindset relates to the mental disciplines and practices required to bring focus to a venture's "big picture" and putting these elements into action. Best practices and disciplines involve developing *capabilities*, such as managing energy and focus, seeking honest and frequent feedback, scanning for opportunities, dealing effectively with risks and adversity, and recharging and balancing one's self. Macro Mindset helps define and determine a venture's *habits of success.*

Micro Mindset produces and guides the specific actions necessary to build a sustainable venture. Micro Mindset focuses on success factors at the level of *behavior*. It determines *ongoing priorities*, such as clarifying purpose and motivation, developing a product or service, generating interest and revenue, growing and aligning an effective team, acquiring relevant resources, expanding a business, creating value for stakeholders and building win-win partnerships that enrich and leverage available resources.

These three overall areas of the Success Mindset Map are comprised of several specific patterns of mindset, behaviors and habits that support the growth of a venture. They are detailed in *The SFM Success Mindset Map™*, which was created in 2016 by Mickey A. Feher and Robert Dilts, with the support of illustrator Antonio Meza. The map provides a very powerful and complete tool to help you focus on the success factors and key elements to observe, define and act upon, in order to best support the growth of a venture through a generative approach. Although we present this tool in depth in this chapter focusing on how to stimulate the growth phase of a venture, it is also useful and significant for surviving crisis and managing transition.

SFM Circle of Success™ Model for Growth

The *SFM Circle of Success™* published in *SFM Vol. 1: Next Generation Entrepreneurs*[4] is about developing and applying an effective entrepreneurial mindset. A "Circle of Success" is constructed by bringing together relevant outcomes, meta mindsets and actions to build a successful and sustainable venture. When working as a generative consultant and leader with organizations in a growth phase, it will be particularly helpful for you to know where to focus your support, since a Circle of Success identifies the five key areas that need to be addressed, strengthened and balanced.

Five core outcomes of a next-generation entrepreneur or venture

The SFM Circle of Success (CoS) focuses on five *core outcomes* to be achieved to make a truly successful and sustainable next- generation venture. They apply as much to you, as a generative consultant or business leader, as to the essential elements you need to for supporting your clients in their own ventures. The outcomes include:

---

4   Robert B. Dilts, *Success Factor Modeling Volume I: Next Generation Entrepreneurs,* Dilts Strategy Group 2017 ASIN: B0743M8BR5

1. Personal Satisfaction
Personal satisfaction is a consequence of connecting with our passion and growing personally and spiritually as a founder, leader and/or entrepreneur.

2. Meaningful Contribution
Making a *meaningful contribution* is rooted in our ability to contribute to society and the environment and foster our own emotional and physical well-being as well as others'.

3. Innovation and Resilience
Innovation and resilience emerge when we link our contribution with the visions and resources of others and ignite new possibilities.

4. Scalable Growth
Scalable growth is a result of leveraging new possibilities and shared visions to build a successful and sustainable venture.

5. Financial Robustness and Profitability
Financial robustness and profitability is the result of connecting our contribution to society and the environment with building a successful and sustainable venture or career.

Achieving the five core outcomes - Key perspectives and critical actions

Peter Senge once said: "Business and human endeavors are systems... we tend to focus on snapshots of isolated parts of the system. And wonder why our deepest problems never get solved."

In order to achieve these outcomes, it is important for a generative consultant to support the leaders of successful ventures to balance their focus of attention and their actions among five fundamental perspectives:

* Self / Identity
* Customers / Market / Products
* Team Members / Employees
* Stakeholders / Investors
* Partners / Alliances

In other words, to attain the five core outcomes for a successful next-generation venture, entrepreneurs and business leaders need to engage in a number of critical actions that include:

1. *Connecting* with **themselves**, with their passion and their *purpose and motivation* for the venture;

2. *Developing products and services* for their **customers** and *generating enough interest and revenue* to support their venture.

3. Growing a **team** of competent members by *creating alignment* with respect to the venture's mission and continuing to *increase their competency* as the business matures;

4. *Raising funds and securing other essential resources* needed to support the venture to reach its ambition, then continuing to *expand the business and create value* for **stakeholders and investors**;

5. *Building win-win relationships* and establishing alliances with strategic **partners** that allow all parties to *enrich and leverage resources* in order to increase visibility and expand their roles in the marketplace.

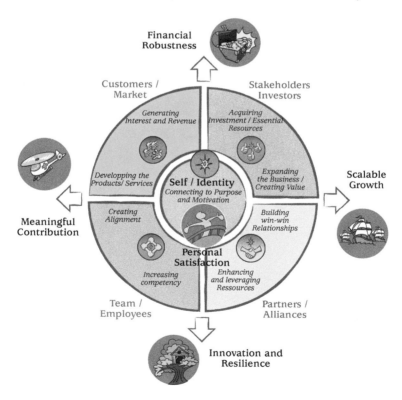

The SFM Circle of Success™ and the Core Outcomes of Next Generation Ventures

The preceding diagram of the Circle of Success implies that **Personal Satisfaction** is central to the success of a generative consultant and business leader. It can be attained by (1) *connecting to purpose and motivation.*

The outcome of **Meaningful Contribution** is primarily achieved through the actions of (2) *developing a product or service* that benefits customers and (3) *creating alignment among team members.*

Achieving the outcome of developing **Innovation and Resilience** is fundamentally a consequence of a business leaders' actions of (4) *increasing the competency* of his or her team members and (5) *enriching and leveraging resources* through partnerships and alliances.

Scalable Growth is predominantly achieved through the actions of (6) *building win-win relationships* with partners and allies and (7) *expanding the business and creating value* for stakeholders and investors.

Financial Robustness is largely the result of the actions of (8) *raising investment and acquiring essential resources* from stakeholders and investors and (9) *generating interest and revenue* from customers.

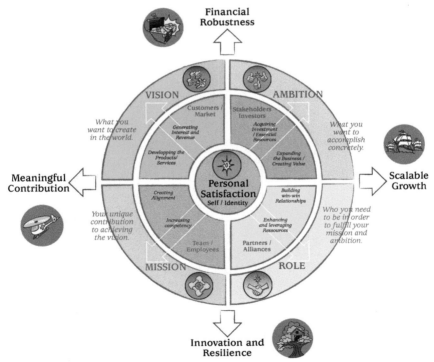

Vision, Mission, Ambition and Role, and the SFM Circle of Success™

Establishing an entrepreneurial mindset

An *entrepreneurial mindset* will produce and encourage the actions necessary to achieve core outcomes. Entrepreneur's develop this mindset through their capacity to share their *passion*, in the form of *vision*, *mission*, *ambition* and *role*, with respect to the key perspectives defined by the Circle of Success.

* Personal *passion* comes from connecting fully with your **self** and your deepest **identity** and discovering what fills you with enthusiasm and energy. It involves exploring the question: *What do you really love to do?*

* Your *vision* is a function of your personal passion expressed outward toward **customers and the market** in order to make a contribution. It is the answer to the question: *What do you want to create in the world?*

* The alignment of **team members and employees** working together to achieve the vision is a result of communicating and sharing your passion in the form of the venture's *mission*. It is a result of answering the question: *What is your unique contribution to the vision?*

* Passion expressed in the form of your *ambition* to build a successful and sustainable venture and create value is what motivates **stakeholders and investors** to offer the resources needed and take the risk to join the venture. It involves being clear about the answer to the question: *What do you want to accomplish concretely?*

* Passion connected to your area of excellence in the form of a *role* from which to build win-win relationships with peers that enrich and leverage resources is what forms the basis for effective **partnerships and alliances**. This requires clarifying: *Who do you need to be in order to fulfill your mission and ambition?*

The most successful ventures are those that produce something that is truly a breakthrough and a "game changing" contribution to the larger socio-economic context, or "field of innovation," in which they exist.

As a consultant in a major corporation in early 2000, I asked the CEO of Cascades Papers: "What keeps you going? What keeps you growing?"

> *"Well, it's not the board room meetings and my accountant [chuckle]...It's about following my intuition. Keep doing what we love to do. Listening and staying connected to the people and our purpose. Creating a creativity-based and eco-responsible culture."*[5]

After pondering his response, I now realize that he embraced the same success factors and entrepreneurial mindsets identified by the SFM Circle of Success. It is not surprising that this corporation was considered in 2019 as part of the top eco-responsible leaders in Canada.[6]

> *"One small step for man...One giant leap for mankind."*
> *– Neil Armstrong (first man on the Moon)*

Determining what needs to grow

The primary challenge of stimulating growth is accelerating the process of change in the right direction. Strategies and tools used to address growth effectively include determining the meta goals of the venture. Meta goals help create the momentum to achieve the venture's desired outcomes. As outlined earlier, you can work as generative consultant with the mindset map and assess key mindsets (meta, macro and micro) that will help your clients succeed in achieving their meta goals.

Intention Setting

The key factors identified in this section will support you in the **second step** of the SFM Generative Consulting DIAMOND Model: **Intention Setting** – Establishing the desired state/direction for change.

---

5   Cascades- Live quote during an interview with President Alain Lemaire

6   https://www.newswire.ca/news-releases/cascades-recognized-for-its-responsible-best-practices-890166687.html

Clarifying Meta Goals

 A *meta goal* is the *current focus* of a project or venture. A person may be working on many important goals at once, but a meta goal is the most important one. A meta goal, or current focus, will relate to one of the five *core outcomes* associated with building a balanced Circle of Success.

As a skillful generative consultant and business leader, you will want to have clarity on your clients' meta goals (see the worksheet on next page). You will support your clients by identifying which of these meta goals require the most focus.

Relational Skills   **Pattern Detection Skills**   **Strategic Thinking Skills**

Your *Relational Skills, Pattern Detection Skills* and *Strategic Skills*[7] will allow you to:

1. Present a situation as factual and interconnected as possible, applying the S.C.O.R.E. model;

2. Identify which key areas of the *Circle of Success* are necessary to stimulate growth;

3. Propose strategies and actions to build an effective *Circle of Success.*

Setting goals is an essential step to turn the invisible into the visible and achieve a venture's desired outcomes. It will allow you to lead the organization in an efficient, holistic and sustainable way, while helping your client's business to achieve scalable growth.

---

7   See self-reflective score cards at the end of the chapter.

Meta Goal assessment

You can use the worksheet below to help your clients and teams assess their ventures' meta goals by rating them from 1 to 5, with 1 being the most important and 5 being the least important. To get a sense of direction, it is useful to identify the current focus and desired focus.

* Which of the following goal(s) best describe your clients' or teams' current focus (CF)?

* Which of the following goal(s) will be the most important for your clients or teams to make progress on in the next six to twelve months in terms of desired focus (DF)?

	Meta Goal	Score	
		CF	**DF**
	1. Increasing your personal satisfaction in what you do – This is represented by a sense of joy, excitement and pleasure in one's ongoing actions and activities. Choose this goal if you are not enthusiastic or excited about what you are doing even if things are going fairly well in your venture.		
	2. Establishing financial robustness/stability – Choose this goal if it is essential for your venture to achieve profitability.		
	3. Building a scalable business – Choose this goal if it is important for your venture to grow, expand groups of units operating together and share a common origin, purpose and mode of coordination.		
	4. Making a genuine and meaningful contribution – Choose this goal if it is important for your venture to clarify and/or enhance the benefits brought to or created for your customers and community.		
	5. Achieving greater innovation and resilience – Choose this goal if you need to increase your capabilities or creativity, in order to adapt to new challenging situations, get through a crisis, deal with a major change or stay competitive.		

It could also be interesting to compare your client's or team's self-assessment with your own expert (outside) assessment, in order to identify possible gaps in perception.

Fish in water do not see the water.
Only once out of water does a fish notice it was in water.

Also note that an emotional state can sometime blur one's perceptions. This makes it important to nourish a generative COACH state, as described in Chapter 1, before doing any kind of evaluation.

2.6 Success Mindset Maps and their generative use in stimulating growth

Meta Mindset – Big-picture clarity

As we have established, *Meta Mindset* relates to success factors at the levels of *purpose* and *identity* and it has to do with our fundamental attitude toward our work, our world and our place in that world. The meta mindset of successful entrepreneurs and leaders is made up of the following six elements. To explore these aspects of meta mindset, reflect upon how clearly you are able to answer the following questions with regards to your clients or /teams. You can assess your client's meta mindset by rating the following six statements on a scale of 0–10 (where 10 is the truest for your client and 0 is not at all true for your client).

Meta Mindset assessment

Meta Mindset	Rating
1. **Do your clients know what they really love to do (know what they are passionate about)?** Passion is an intense desire or enthusiasm for something. It is a relentless inner drive to find what one cares deeply about and wishes to pursue with all of his or her heart.	0 - 10
2. **Do your clients know what they want to help create in the future (are clear about their destinations and their long-term visions)?** Vision can best be defined as "a mental image of what the future will or could be like." The creative vision of successful entrepreneurs has to do with the ability to imagine and focus on long-term possibilities that improve people's lives in some way. It involves the ability to see beyond the confines of the "here and now" and imagine future scenarios. It also involves the capacity to set and stay focused on long-term goals, and adopting long-term plans and a holistic view.	0 - 10

	Meta Mindset	Rating
	3. Are your clients clear about their direction, regardless of whether or not they know the ultimate destination? Vision is about looking into the future to see what one wants to create in the world through a venture. However, one cannot always see the final result so clearly when looking that far ahead. Sometimes an entrepreneur has a direction in mind, but not a specific end-goal or destination.	0 - 10
	4. Do your clients know their purpose (know what they stand for and why they are doing what they are doing)?. Are they clear about their mission – the unique contribution they want to make through their venture? The mission of an individual or organization has to do with their contribution to manifesting a particular vision. It relates to the unique gift and contribution brought to the table to realize a vision. The mission of an individual within an organization has to do with his or her contribution to that organization and its vision. Similarly, an organization's mission will be with respect to the larger system of its customers and their needs. .	0 - 10
	5. Are your clients clear about their ambitions – what do they want to become and achieve in the next two to five years)? Ambition is a result of the desire and determination to achieve success and self-recognition. Ambition is defined as "a strong desire to do or achieve something, typically requiring determination and hard work", which provides personal benefit. Ambitions arise in the form of dreams and aspirations. A healthy ego comes from the drive for growth and mastery. .	0 - 10
	6. Are your clients clear about their roles within the organization and the position they have with respect to others in their markets/environments? Role is defined as "the function assumed or part played by a person in a particular situation." A "function" is based upon competency, while "the part played" is determined by one's position or status. On the one hand, a role reflects personal skills, abilities and efforts and is related to what a person does (or is expected to do). On the other hand, role reflects "status"; i.e. who one is in relation to others. Therefore, role is an intersection of both the position a person occupies with respect to others and the expected capabilities and behaviors attached to that position.	0 - 10

Action Planning

Now, reflect on the scores. Which ones are below a rating of 7/10? These are areas for potential improvement. They may even be essential areas for improvement depending upon your client's' meta goals for their ventures or yours as a business leader. We invite you to explore these areas further with your clients, as they will be useful to identify key actions to be included in the **third step** of the SFM Generative Consulting DIAMOND Model: **Action Planning** – *Building a critical path.*

Questions to consider for Action Planning

1. Passion
- *What do your clients really love to do?*
- *What are they excited about?*
- *What is interesting and compelling for them?*
- *What brings them a deep sense of enthusiasm and energy?*

2. Long-term Vision
- *What do your clients want to create in the world through their venture?*
- *What new possibilities do they want to see in the world?*
- *What is the world to which they want to belong?*

3. Direction
- *What do your clients want to see improved or different in the world?*
- *What do they want to see more of and less of in the future?*

4. Purpose and Mission
- *What is your clients' service to the larger system and vision?*
- *What is their unique contribution to making the vision happen?*
- *What special gifts, resources, capabilities and actions do they bring to the larger system to help achieve the vision?*

5. Ambition
- *What type of lives do your clients want to create for themselves?*
- *What do they want to accomplish? What type of status and performance do they want to achieve for themselves and others?*
- *What would they like to be recognized and/or remembered for? What would they like to add to their resume or biography?*

6. Role
- *What type of person do your clients need to be and role do they need to have in order to create the life that they want and succeed in their ambitions? Missions? Visions?*
- *What is their positions with respect to others in their environment/market?*
- *What core competences are necessary to become the type of person that they need to be or achieve and remain in the necessary positions or status?*

Macro Mindset – Habits of success

As stated previously, macro mindset relates to the mental disciplines and practices required to bring focus to the big picture of a venture and begins to put it into action. Such practices strengthen the mental discipline necessary for sustainable success. These involve such capabilities as managing one's energy and focus, seeking honest and frequent feedback, scanning for opportunities, dealing effectively with risks and adversity, and recharging and balancing oneself.

The macro mindset of successful entrepreneurs and leaders is made up of the following five "habits of success." Assess yours and your clients' macro mindset by rating the following five statements on a scale of 0–10 (where 10 is the truest and 0 is not true). As a generative business leader and/or consultant, you may want to answer these questions by putting yourself in second position or third position, or even directly interviewing your clients or your team.

Macro Mindset assessment

	Macro Mindset	Rating
	1. **Doing what one is passionate about and investing a lot of energy and focus into making what is wanted to happen.** This is an essential attribute needed to begin or to complete any entrepreneurial endeavor.	0 - 10
	2. **Seeking feedback and establishing ways to get honest and frequent feedback.** Getting honest and frequent feedback is an important habit of success in order to avoid problems and obstacles and make necessary course corrections.	0 - 10
	3. **Constantly scanning for opportunities and investing time to create them.** Consistently scanning one's horizon for possibilities and "weak signals" that may indicate important opportunities. This is a key characteristic of all successful entrepreneurs.	0 - 10
	4. **Being internally grounded and resourceful and having ways of recharging and balancing oneself and practice them on a daily basis.** Having the means and the discipline to take care of oneself and not become overly stressed or burned out. Using practices that help to ground, balance and recharge is an essential aspect of sustained and healthy success..	0 - 10
	5. **Being aware of risks and potential problems and not getting discouraged or distracted in the face of adversity and negative feedback.** Having the tools and resources to remain in control under challenging and changing conditions. Being able to remain focused and "stay the course" is one of the most important attributes of successful entrepreneurs. One must know how to "seize the helm" and steer through stormy waters.	0 - 10

Once again, reflect on the scores given above. Which ones are below 7/10? Take note these lower ratings in your macro mindset and start exploring ways to improve them. These are areas for potential improvement. And, as with the various elements of your clients' meta mindset, they will be essential areas for improvement relating to your clients' or teams' meta goals.

Action Planning

Exploring how to improve these habits of success will help you to identify key actions to address in the third step of the SFM Generative Consulting DIAMOND Model: **Action Planning** – Building a critical path. This frequently involves incorporating multiple levels of change.

Generative consulting toolkit -- Developing habits of success

While working on the first (*Defining Present State*) and second (*Intention Setting*) steps of the SFM Generative Consulting DIAMOND Model, – it might be easy to identify many elements to work on at once. But, as you know, aiming everywhere will get you nowhere. It may be best to prioritize elements to be concentrated on. To best support yours or your client's' projects, you will want to create your own generative consultant toolkit.

Here is an example of an effective tool to add to your toolkit. It will help you determine initiatives to prioritize for effective *Action Planning.*

Prioritizing Initiatives

It can be hard to identify which projects to eliminate and which to re-focus. The following matrix provides an approach to assessing current projects or actions, with a view to stopping lower-value initiatives, and reassigning resources to higher-value ones.

* Start by taking an inventory of major ongoing initiatives. Divide them into an A, B and C list based on the number of people and resources they are using and the size of their anticipated benefit.

* Take the A list of projects and, for each project, estimate the following:

   - The benefit expected (high, medium, low)

   - The time period in which the benefit can be achieved (short-, medium- or long-term)

   - The feasibility of implementation (high, medium, low)

   - The investment required to achieve the benefit ($)

* Map each project or action in the matrix shown below.

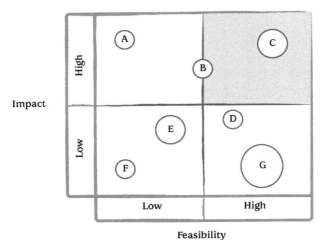

Feasibility

* Combine the benefit and time period into one average high/medium/low rating for each project or action. Use the size of investment required to deliver the benefit as the size of the bubble identifying each project or action.

  - For example: if you intend to move the business to another location to enhance visibility, attract more clients, increase output capacity and have an environment adapted to your teams' needs and criteria and you consider this as having a high impact/benefit on the short-term, medium feasibility to implement and high costs, you would draw a large circle in the upper quadrant close to the mid-section located near "B" in the diagram above.

  - Note: You could also awaken your multiple intelligences and be generative by using symbols or metaphors to illustrate each project in the matrix.

* Do the same on separate matrices for B and C projects or actions. Then working with a multi-disciplinary team, devise a strategy for each project or action. Determine if you will eliminate, refocus, merge or refresh it by adding resources. You can track each project over time to make sure that these strategies are implemented. Old projects sometimes take a long time to die out and can resurface in different guises. Make process or policy changes as necessary.

What other tools would you add to your toolkit to support your or your clients' projects in developing a **Macro Mindset?**

_____

_____

_____

_____

_____

Micro Mindset – Ongoing Priorities

 As we have established, a Micro Mindset provides and guides the specific actions necessary to build a sustainable venture. The micro mindset of successful entrepreneurs and leaders is a function of identifying their ongoing priorities.

The micro mindset of successful entrepreneurs and leaders is defined with respect to nine critical actions.

 1. **SelfMotivator:** Setting aside the time to explore and reconnect with what you love to do, what is important to you and what you are good at doing – i.e., your passion, your sense of purpose and your excellence.

 2. **MarketMaker:** Creating opportunities for ongoing dialog with customers and prospects – The focus of the MarketMaker mindset is to open and maintain dialog with multiple customers and customer representatives in order to generate interest and revenue.

 3. **ProductCreator:** Brainstorming, generating and implementing products, solutions and services that anticipate and fulfill customer needs – The ProductCreator mindset aims to anticipate and fulfill customer needs and desires by developing innovative and empowering solutions (products and services).

 4. **TeamMaker:** Attracting and providing direction and support to team members, and encouraging team cooperation – The emphasis of the TeamMaker mindset is to attract and give direction to people who support the venture's mission (its products and services) by fostering synergy, complementarity and alignment.

5. **CompetenceBuilder:** Encouraging team members and providing them with opportunities to learn and grow – The primary focus of the CompetenceBuilder mindset is on providing opportunities and resources necessary for team members to grow and to increase competency.

6. **FinanSourcerer:** Identifying potential investors and providers of other essential resources and creatively securing their interest and commitment to support your venture – The priority of the FinanSourcerer mindset is to identify sources of funding and other essential resources (stakeholders and investors) and creatively connect them to the venture's ambitions and strengths.

7. **VentureBuilder:** Creating and developing a sustainable infrastructure and a path to growth and scalability for your venture – The VentureBuilder mindset concentrates on establishing a sustainable infrastructure and a path to growth and scalability for the venture, in order to create value for investors and other stakeholders.

8. **MatchMaker:** Seeking and establishing win-win relationships with potential partners and allies who resonate with your values and vision – The purpose of the MatchMaker mindset is to seek other ventures (partners/alliances) that share common visions and values and complement one another's roles and strengths (through sharing, combining or exchanging), in order to build win-win relationships.

9. **ReSourcerer:** Identifying and leveraging synergies between you are doing and the products, services or competences of other ventures – . The primary concern of the Resourcerer mindset is to recognize, explore and implement significant synergies with the products, services, competences, etc., of other complementary ventures (partners/alliances), in order to enrich and leverage resources.

Micro Mindset Assessment

This next questionnaire will help you identify the micro mindsets to address. You may self-reflect as a generative business leader or consultant with your own clients or use it with an outside perspective when you assess a team or business.

Micro Mindset	I, we, he, she or they enjoy(s) it	I, we, he, she or they (am/is) are good at it	I, we, he, she or they (am/is) are spending time doing it
1. Setting aside the time to explore and reconnect with what you love to do, what is important to you and what you are good at doing –i.e., your passion, your sense of purpose and your excellence.			
2. Creating opportunities for ongoing dialog with customers and prospects.			
3. Brainstorming and implementing products and services that anticipate and fulfill customer needs.			
4. Attracting and providing direction and support to team members and encouraging team cooperation.			
5. Encouraging team members and providing them with opportunities to learn and grow.			
6. Identifying potential investors and providers of other essential resources and creatively securing their interest and commitment to support your venture.			
7. Creating and developing a sustainable infrastructure and a path to growth and scalability for your venture.			
8. Seeking and establishing win-win relationships with potential partners and allies who resonate with your values and vision.			
9. Identifying and leveraging synergies between what you are doing and the products, services or competences of other ventures.			

Put an "X" in the columns that best fit your clients' or your teams' self-reflection, with respect to the actions in the table.

This time, as you reflect on the answers given above, be aware of the different aspects of mindset that various responses represent.

* If one enjoys the activity, is good at it and spends time doing it, then it is clearly a strength. However, that strength could be an asset or a limitation depending on whether or not it is the most important thing to do to reach current goals for the venture.

* If one enjoys the activity and is good at it but does not spend time doing it, then it probably means priorities are given to other actions. In this case, the main question is whether or not one should spend time in this activity to reach the project's or venture's goal.

* If one enjoys the activity and spends time doing it but is not good at it, then it is likely a source of frustration. It would be good to get some training or coaching for this activity.

* If one is good at the activity and spends time doing it but does not enjoy it, then one probably experiences it as necessary, but tedious and boring. It would be useful to explore ways to increase personal motivation. For instance, it can be helpful to spend time with and model someone who genuinely enjoys doing it.

* If one enjoys the activity but is not good at it and does not spend time doing it, then it probably does not add much value even though one takes pleasure in it. It is definitely something one will need to invest time to learn more about and improve upon, depending on the venture's goals.

* If one spends time doing the activity but does not enjoy it and is not good at it, then one will likely feel frequently overwhelmed and find oneself "spinning one's wheels" or wasting time, even if one thinks that the activity is important to do. This is clearly an area one needs to get support in developing both capability and motivation.

* If one is good at the activity but neither likes it nor spends time doing it, then it is clearly an issue of motivation rather than one of competency or priority. It would be useful to spend some time to gain a better understanding of the reasons why the activity is important and explore how one might increase interest and pleasure in doing it.

* If one does not enjoy the activity, is not good at it and does not spend time doing it, then it is an obvious area for development. One will need some serious support to develop motivation and capability in that area, or find a good, partner that can be trusted who has competence in that activity.

Again, take note of most important areas for development.

Generative consulting toolkit - Supporting Macro-Mindset development

Prioritizing tasks

Entrepreneurs, leaders and managers frequently have to select and prioritize their activities and initiatives. According to the 80/20 rule, managers would want to focus on the 20 % of the actions or initiatives that produce 80 % of the results. The following tool provides an approach to explore and identify initiatives that are likely to be the most significant and have the greatest leverage in reaching longer-term results. On the left-hand side of the table, list the initiatives that yourself, as a business leader, or your client must prioritize or from which to select. Then, rate the degree to which each initiative matches (high, medium or low) the six decision criteria listed across the top of the table.

* **Mission Critical:** How significant is the initiative with respect to your group's or organization's mission?

* **Congruent with Key Values:** How fully does the initiative match your group's or organization's key values?

* **Matches Core Competence:** To what extent does the initiative fit with your group's or organization's core competences?

* **Fits with Critical Success Factors:** To what extent does the initiative meet key success factors? (e.g., clear need, adequate sponsorship, stakeholder buy-in, tangible feedback, etc.)

* **Degree of Payoff:** What is the potential payoff of the initiative?

* **Amount of Cost/Risk:** How much cost or risk is associated with the initiative?

One way to quickly tally the results is to assign a number (3–High, 2–Medium, 1–Low) to each rating (make the number associated with cost/risk a negative number) and add them up.

Decision Criteria
(Rate as H = High, M = Medium, L = Low)

Initiatives	Mission Critical	Congruent with Key Values	Matches Core Competences	Fits with Critical Success Factors	Degree of Payoff	Amount of Cost/Risk

What other tools would you add to your toolkit to support your or your client's projects in developing Micro Mindset?

_____

_____

_____

SFM Success MindsetMap™

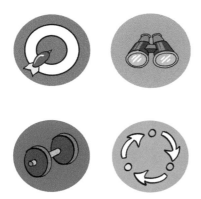

Putting all the pieces—Meta Goals, Meta Mindset, Macro Mindset and Micro Mindset—together with respect to the Circle of Success can be summarized in the overall *SFM Success MindsetMap™*. Many elements are intertwined.

The SFM Success MindsetMap™ refers to the specific aspects of mindset that are needed to achieve the various core outcomes defined by the Circle of Success. For instance, securing financial robustness would require a different combination of Meta, Macro and Micro Mindset attributes than the mindset for, say, increasing innovation and resilience.

Thus, similar to a literal map, the SFM Success MindsetMap™, created by Mickey A. Feher and Robert Dilts, shows which course to take if you want or need to move your clients' project or venture in a certain direction.

In summary, the SFM Success MindsetMap™ specifies which elements of the three areas of mindset—Meta, Macro and Micro— are the most important and relevant for achieving the various core outcomes defined by the Circle of Success. Depending on your *meta goal* or *current focus* for your venture, an outcome could be enhancing personal satisfaction, making a meaningful contribution, securing financial robustness, increasing innovation and resilience or achieving scalable growth. The SFM Success MindsetMap™ helps you to identify your clients' particular aptitudes and tendencies and to know which ones you and your clients need to prioritize and strengthen, in order to take your clients' project or venture to the next level.

By assessing the three areas of mindset— Meta, Macro and Micro— with respect to the Meta Goal, the SFM Success MindsetMap™ will help you to specify which elements of the three areas of mindset are the most important and relevant for achieving the venture's meta goal or current focus, by providing you with an *Ideal Mindset Map* for that meta goal.

As you have in the preceding pages gone through the various mindset assessments with a left-brain perspective, it could also be very enriching to use multiple intelligences to refine answers. You could use symbols, metaphors, gestures and sounds to become even more familiar with your teams' or your clients' particular aptitudes and tendencies, with respect to your or their current mindsets, skills and habits. Once this is done, you may then compare responses with the Ideal Mindset Map for their meta goals. You will discover which ones need to be prioritized and strengthened in order to take the project or venture to the next level.

To find the Ideal Mindset Map for each Meta Goal, we invite you to visit: **www.mindsetmaps.com.**

And to get an example of how this map is used in a real case, we invite you to read Mickey's Chapter 6. In this chapter, he describes how he used the SFM Success Mindset Map to assist one of his clients to shift his mindset, in order to transform himself, his team and his company.

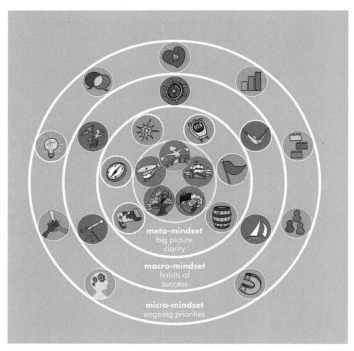

This is the whole Mindset Map system. You can find your personal Mindset Map in www.mindset-maps.com

2.7 Growth and the seven steps of generative consulting - Application example

In this chapter, we have shown how to use the SFM Circle of Success (CoS) as a core model to support the first three steps of the generative consulting process and shared some additional tools for the other steps. As a generative consultant, your generativity, knowledge and experiences will enable you to create your own toolkit to follow through on each step of the SFM Generative Consulting DIAMOND Model process.

As Robert points out in Chapter 1, consulting can take days, weeks or even months. Although the first three steps of the SFM DIAMOND Model can advance fairly quickly, the fourth step – the implementation phase – can take many months. Your role as a generative consultant and business leader is to develop a program and roadmap for your clients or teams to integrate multiple interventions, in order to achieve key organizational outcomes that have potentially never been achieved before. As a reminder, your main focus is on the process rather than on the content. You do not need to be a "content expert" to guide people through processes that apply the use of multiple intelligences, in order to help them to maximize their own resources and use their imaginations to come up with strategic and optimizing solutions.

I like to be inspired by entrepreneurial success stories. I will share here a story that I learned at the NLP Leadership summit in Alicante, Spain, in January 2020. The amazing synchronicity was that this person passionately shared how SFM and the processes developed by Robert and his late brother John have contributed to the growth and success of two of his own businesses. As he said: *"There was a before SFM and then there is an after."* You will find in Appendix II the full inspirational story of MailNinja, one of Tony Nutley's businesses, and how it all started and evolved into a "zero to hero" example. Through an interview and generative exchange that I had with him, you will get a taste of how the SFM Generative Consulting DIAMOND Model was applied and continues to stimulate the growth of his business.

In a nutshell: MailNinja started in 2005, in Swindon, U.K., with Doug Dennison as CEO and Tony Nutley as COO. In 15 years, they built an email agency that went from nothing to nine employees with a yearly turnover of almost a million pounds.

Here is the synthesis of how the S.C.O.R.E. and CoS were applied in support of MailNinja's generative success:

S.C.O.R.E Overview

Market and Personal Symptoms	Possible Causes		Desired Outcomes	Possible Resources
	Outer	Inner		
• Small- to medium-sized businesses have trouble with email marketing • Doug was no longer happy in his previous job and took a course in email marketing	• Lack of time and adequate resources	• Lack of training and know-how	• Create a useful and effective ESP- Email Service Provider company	• Explore Doug's passions • Create a compelling vision for business • Set ambitions • Build a team) • Find partners • Develop a balanced Circle of Success

MailNinja's Roadmap to success in a nutshell – How was the SFM Circle of Success applied?

1. They implemented the SFM Circle of Success (CoS) with Doug at the center of it all.
   - *We explored -* **Who** *is this person was and what is his passion.*
   - *We determined -* **How** *we are going to enable that passion to express along the logical levels.*
   - *We identified -* **Where** *would be the gap that's going to cause us some pain.*

2. Then they crystallized what kind of customers they wanted:
   - *Small-to-medium-sized business owners and all the marketing managers in slightly larger enterprises.*

3. They identified who would make up the team that they needed and built it:
   - *We had to hire people because we could not do it all ourselves.*
   - *We have invested a huge amount of money in supporting our team members through training, development support and out-of-work initiatives.*

4. They found the stakeholders that they needed:
   - *HSBC – This bank became the main stakeholder, because they fronted some money for us, which was very nice of them to do that. Thanks very much, HSBC!*

5. They established effective partnerships:
   - *We partnered with MailChimp, the largest email service provider in the world, with whom we now have a fantastic win-win and mutually supportive relationship.*
   - *We also partnered with a couple of other key people and software organizations who were very, very supportive.*

6. They planned and moved into action:
   - *We determined our vision and ambition.*

7. They transformed obstacles to stay on track, keep focus and stick to their plan:
   - *We make sure that there are regular checks and balances so that we do not lose our way.*

To read more and get the full version of how the SFM DIAMOND Model was implemented, **see Appendix II**. May Tony's story inspire you in your own venture and provide effective guidelines for your clients' ventures.

Vision: To add value to small-to medium-sized businesses and help them grow significantly

Ambition: To be the number one Email Service Supporter in the U.K. and have a worldwide customer base, sending out millions of emails and making a million and a half-ton of business by the end of the year (2020)

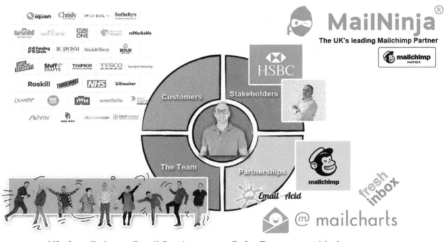

Mission: To be an Email Service Provider and do email marketing; to support people who use MailChimp as their preferred ESP

Role: To partner with the largest Email Service Provider (ESP) in the world – MailChimp

MailNinja- Circle of Success

2.9 Competences for Stimulating Growth

Essential competences for any generative consultant and business leader include to be continuously curious, creative and flexible. The ability to use multiple intelligences (visual, somatic, metaphorical, collective, etc.) in order to define a Circle of Success maximizes your chances of getting the richest and most comprehensive perspective of your clients' situations and challenges. In addition to these competences, there are key skills to integrate specifically while working with clients' businesses or your own in a growth phase.

One of the key competencies for any entrepreneur, leader and generative consultant to promote growth is a very high level of relational skills.

* **Relational Skills** – the ability to establish rapport and create trust. An effective consultant needs to be able to establish trusting relationships with clients for there to be meaningful change. Without trust, people are unwilling to try something new and take risks.

To be effective at creating a program and pathway for your clients, your pattern detection skills and ability to think strategically will also be essential.

* **Pattern Detection Skills** – the ability to spot both strong and weak signals on different levels of trends and meaning in data, business ecosystem and interpersonal interactions.

* **Strategic Thinking** – the ability to work on both ambition and vision (meaning and purpose) and see how smaller steps create a critical path to a larger outcome.

How do you rate with respect to these three key competences?

The following questions will help you self-reflect on your own abilities. Your responses can give you valuable cues about what you can personally focus and work on with your next client.

Self-evaluation Questions

a) Relational Skills

1. What did you do to build trust and create an environment of psychological safety with your client?

2. How frequently did you acknowledge your client's feedback, concerns and ideas?

3. In what way did you adjust your language and timing to pace and match that of your client's?

b) Pattern Detection Skills

1. On which levels (environment, behavior, capabilities, values and beliefs, identity and purpose) did you observe potential patterns with regard to the SFM Circle of Success?

2. What kind of links did you make between information given and your personal observations?

3. How did you integrate different levels of information drawn from data, your client's business ecosystem and interpersonal interactions to find key patterns?

c) Strategic Thinking

1. How did you ensure that your client was not only focusing on the next steps (short-term objectives), but also keeping consistent attention on the bigger picture (longer-term direction)?

2. How did you ensure that your client's ambitions were aligned with the larger vision?

3. How did you use both details and knowledge about the bigger picture to build a critical path leading to both the ambition and the vision?

2.10 Key takeaways for this chapter

Stimulating growth is a necessary step to ensure a venture's successful and sustainable future. The role you will play as a generative consultant and business leader is of the utmost importance to achieve this purpose. To summarize, to help your clients and teams build a robust SFM Circle of Success™, you will support them to:

* Connect to their passion and purpose;

* Formulate an inspiring long-term vision (human-centered, systemic and authentic) and communicate it with charisma;

* Create a product or service that meets their customers' needs;

* Create alignment by identifying a mission that supports their vision;

* Set clear goals and ambitions which are measurable and balanced with their vision;

* Raise investment and acquire essential resources to successfully move forward;

* Enhance and leverage their resources and talents and define clear roles in their business venture;

* Build win-win relationships in the venture and with partners, collaborators, stakeholders and customers.

When we, as generative consultants and business leaders, are ourselves able to "be the change" that our clients want to see, we become influential catalysts for their success.

Through my own experience, I find that we best support our clients through our own personal and professional growth (see Chapter 6 – Be Generative). May this chapter on stimulating growth and the chapters ahead provide guidance and clarity for you to find your own opportunities and possible expansions, in order to move forward to a new level of success.

Once a robust Circle of Success is achieved, your clients will be on the roadway to generative success. Your last task and eighth 'unofficial' step will be to celebrate!

May you be the generative change you want to see
in your clients' lives and businesses.

May your clients' ventures, and your own,
live long and prosper.

A crisis (from the Greek κρίσις - krisis; adjectival form: "critical") is any event that is going (or is expected) to lead to an unstable and dangerous situation affecting an individual, group, community, or whole society. Crises are deemed to be negative changes in the security, economic, political, societal, or environmental affairs, especially when they occur abruptly, with little or no warning.

https://en.wikipedia.org/wiki/Crisis

Chapter 3

How to generatively manage crisis in business

Kathrin M. Wyss and Robert B. Dilts

3.1 Overview

In situations of crisis it is important to quickly support the organization to achieve results, create and manage change, develop people and realize values. In this chapter we will focus on how as generative consultants and business leaders you can use the *SFM Leadership Model* and the SFM DIAMOND Model to do so. In Chapter 2 we shared the key areas for success that any business can achieve by applying the SFM Circle of Success™ and the SFM Success MindsetMap. In this chapter we want to build on all those areas and focus specifically on how leadership plays an important role in steering and guiding the current (business) world, as it becomes more and more volatile, uncertain, complex and ambiguous (VUCA).

3.2 Why is this chapter important ?

Leadership is the process by which a person sets a purpose for others and motivates them to pursue it with effectiveness and full commitment. As a result, leadership transforms individual potential into collective performance. In 2008 Rakesh Khurana and Nitin Nohria postulated in their article *It's Time to Make Management a True Profession*[1] that, "when we build our business in a conscious way, it becomes easier to remember our intention (passion aligned with vision) and question the status quo (mission, ambition, role)." By analyzing the leadership culture of an organization through the filter of the SFM Leadership Model in the first step of the generative consulting DIAMOND process (*Defining Present State*) through the perspectives of the SFM Leadership Model, leaders and generative consultants will find key anchor points for change management initiatives that can get the collective performance back on track. Such change initiatives can best be implemented by applying the principles of the SFM Collective Intelligence Model that will be further discussed in Chapter 4.

---

1   Hippocratic path for managers 2008 HBR 86 no 10 70-77
    https://hbr.org/2008/10/its-time-to-make-management-a-true-profession

3.3 Setting the context

Before delving into the SFM Leadership Model, let us look at this context through the filters of current philosophies, trends and employee's expectations regarding good leadership.

Over the last two decades a new business paradigm has evolved and accelerated since *Generation Y* (more often referred to as *millennials*) has begun entering the workforce. While many old school CEOs are being perceived and criticized as greedy, truly visionary leaders such as Elon Musk and Richard Branson believe in a vision and goals that benefit themselves as well as others. They understand that it is the leader's vision and "soul" that attract loyal employees willing to go above and beyond the call of corporate duty. This realization aligns with the needs and desires of millennials, as described by the majority of research. Millennials have a preference for a flat corporate culture, expect close working relationships and frequent feedback from their supervisors. They also place an emphasis on work-life balance and social consciousness[2,3].

We are today working in an age in which business and work have replaced religion and politics as the central forces in contemporary life. This makes it paramount for many people, and especially the millennials, to find their contribution at work, not only for their own happiness, but also to create a just and evolving society. In his book '*Good Business: Leadership, Flow, and the Making of Meaning*'[4] Mihaly Csikszentmihalyi shares that humans cannot survive without hope and identifies three crucial factors to operate a good business:

1. Trust,

2. Commitment to fostering the personal growth of employees,

3. Dedication to creating products that help mankind.

2   Myers, Karen K.; Sadaghiani, Kamyab (1 January 2010). "Millennials in the Work place: A Communication Perspective on Millennials' Organizational Relationships and Performance". *Journal of Business and Psychology.* 25 (2): 225–238.

3   Hershatter, Andrea; Epstein, Molly (1 January 2010). "Millennials and the World of Work: An Organization and Management Perspective". *Journal of Business and Psychology.* 25 (2): 211–223

4   Mihaly Csikszentmihalyi. *Good Business: leadership, flow and the making of meaning,* Penguin Books 2004, ISBN 9780142004098

Daniel Pink asserts in his 2009 book *'Drive: The surprising truth about what motivates us'*[5] that businesses which only focus on profits without valuing purpose will end up with poor customer service and unhappy employees. Pink sees three similar factors as essential in order to motivate employees to perform beyond their basic tasks and to increase their performance and satisfaction:

1. Autonomy – the desire to be self-directed to increase engagement over compliance,

2. Mastery – the urge to be better skilled,

3. Purpose – the desire to do something that has meaning and is important.

3.4 The importance of conscious leadership in crisis

What makes this all so vital to have in mind when looking into how to best survive crisis? In many crisis situations, the old ways and linear thinking don't work anymore. What used to be effective, no longer produces successful results and may even make things worse. More often than not, crisis situations go in line with financial ruptures or constraints which fuel the need to reduce expenses, recover sales and/or customers, or recover public image in order to stop the depletion of sales. To do so effectively and swiftly, the whole organization needs to understand the situation, and take aligned actions in order to develop new products, reengineer processes, reduce waste, etc.

It therefore becomes necessary, in surviving crisis, to encourage the workforce to give their best level performance in order to create a whole new way of doing things. Yet more often than not, this is not the natural response. Employees, who are human beings by nature, deal with crisis as individuals in many different ways. The workforce as a whole often becomes anxious, loses trust in the organization's ability to secure a safe workplace and/or becomes uncomfortable with changes that need to be implemented in a timely if not urgent manner. Worries and concerns are at the forefront of people's attention, they lose focus on effectiveness, performance levels drop, and some people might even disengage due to excessively high stress levels. All those factors make it indeed mandatory that, during a time of crisis, a special focus must be given to developing and strengthening all aspects of *conscious leadership* and *resilience*.

---

5   Daniel H. Pink, *Drive: The surprising truth about what motivates us*. Riverhead Books, 2009 ISBN: 978-1594488849

"Leadership is not being in charge; Leadership is about taking care of those in your charge."

-- Simon Sinek

3.5 How to start tackling a crisis in a generative way

Some say that in a crisis situation you need a "cool head and a warm heart." In other words, you need to stay focused on relevant issues AND connected to the people involved, giving both equal importance.

As a coach or practitioner working with an individual-centric approach, you would focus on self-leadership and individual resilience. As a generative consultant or business leader, your interest and duty lie in focusing and reflecting on how to best instill understanding, readiness and ability for change to a group of many team members, many teams, many different functions, many different offices or subsidiaries, and maybe even many different time zones, countries and cultures. This adds up to a fair amount of complexity.

Yet, refocusing the crisis situation back to a few single targets by defining what needs to be done and identifying how to best do it from a generative mindset allows you to map a path of change. In any crisis, the frequent evaluation of progress through the facets of the SFM DIAMOND Model is important. In particular Facet 6 – Noting Progress – is key to steer the process once you have a solid base through a comprehensive assessment of the current situation (Facet 1 – Defining Present State) and have set the horizon for change (Facet 2 – Intention Setting).

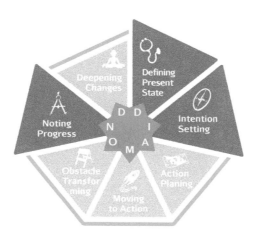

The SFM Circle of Success, described in depth in the previous chapter, provides a great reference for information gathering during the first two facets of the SFM DIAMOND Model. It can help you determine if the source of the crisis is related to:

* the customers or market with regard the organization's products or services

* the team, such as when the organization has an unstable workforce who have no trust in management

* the organization's financial stability or its reputation with stakeholders

* the loss of key partners (internal or external) which can prevent the organization from fulfilling important roles and functions

In any such situation, especially if the crisis involves more than one area of the Circle of Success, the first aim of a consulting process is to bring awareness of what is happening rapidly and effectively into the system. By listening and reflecting what you hear and clarifying your take on the information you have gathered, you need to sort out all aspects with respect their connection with the S.C.O.R.E. model. As shown in Chapter 1, this allows you to categorize aspects as:

* events from the past that might be related to the cause (C) of the crisis

* the present expression of its symptoms (S) and then

* the outcome (O) and the desired effect (E) anticipated as a result of achieving the outcome.

The following table gives an example of some of the typical factors that you might encounter during a crisis situation.

Surviving Crisis

Symptoms	Possible Causes		Desired Outcomes	Possible Resources
	Outer	**Inner**		
• Loss of revenues, reserves and funding. • Loss of confidence, motivation and productivity. • Inability to fulfill fundamental mission.	• Receding economy. • Market decline/collapse. • Decline in company life-cycle. • Uncertainty.	• CRASH • Caught in survival strategies. • Inappropriate leadership strategy. • Loss of vision. • Too much Critic.	• Reduce waste and expenses • Reengineer processes • Recover sales, customers, etc. • Major course correction / pivot. • Innovation at all levels.	• Reinvent, renew and reinforce. • Find partners. • Conscious and emotionally intelligent leadership. • Alignment to vision and clear values. • Making decisions, communicating decisions, configuring people and implementing decisions..

It is not uncommon in a situation of crisis, however, for different stakeholders to have different and divergent perspectives which can be distorted by their subjective emotional responses. The ability to shed light on the source of a particular crisis by structuring information and bringing insight can significantly reduce the level of arousal and the degree of emotional attachment. It can also clarify connections that have not yet been grasped or understood. By doing so, it increases people's potential for creativity and strategic thinking. In times of crisis, people are frequently caught in their assumptions, various types of negative thoughts or in making accusations about who is responsible for the "disaster/crisis."

Pattern detection

Strategic thinking

Emotional intelligence

Systemic thinking

In such situations, it is important to apply relevant tools and to utilize multiple intelligences in order to fortify your expertise as a generative consultant. This especially involves focusing on the skills of *Pattern detection skills*, *Emotional intelligence* (in order to address the "shadows" in the room) and *Strategic* and *Systemic thinking* abilities.

In my experience over the last decade, one of the most useful approaches to address the "shadows in the room" is to use metaphors and images to talk about "what is not going well" (Facet 1 – Defining Present State) or what is a desired outcome (Facet 2 – Intention Setting). While there are many visual aid cards available in different formats for purchase, I find it a very valuable exercise to let teams work on their own individual collages and present them to their peers. In this way, everyone can express in their own style how they understand the current challenge and what kind of hopes they have for solutions. And as a generative consultant or business leader, you can elicit some useful metaphors and emotional catch phrases that can consequently be utilized throughout the whole process of addressing the crisis. This is indeed very useful; as the more ways you can address and talk about the process of change using language that speaks to and includes the emotional state of all of the relevant actors, the more success you will achieve.

To talk about "what is not going well" (Defining Present State) and about what is the "desired outcome" (Intention Setting) are very useful practices to start the process of Generative Consulting for surviving crisis.

To briefly summarize, applying these competences allows you to:

1. present the situation as factually and interconnected as possible using the S.C.O.R.E. model

2. identify, using the SFM Circle of Success, the key areas of focus to tackle the crisis

3. creatively find implementation options with respect to the key strategies outlined in the SFM Leadership Model (to follow) for how to effectively engage the team.

This enables you to lead the organization or the team through the crisis in an efficient, holistic and sustainable way.

3.6 The SFM Leadership Model™ for Conscious Leadership and Resilience

In a situation of crisis, the SFM Leadership Model™ as presented in *SFM Vol. 3: Conscious Leadership and Resilience*[6] is very helpful to plot three key areas of challenge that need to be addressed and balanced during times of high-level stress.

I. **System Leadership** – focusing on effectively promoting change and achieving results.

II. **Leading-Others-Leadership** – embracing the development of people and the realization of key values.

III. **Self-Leadership** – addressing the inner game and personal resilience of the key individuals involved in the change.

Fig. 1 The SFM Leadership Model™

6   Robert B. Dilts, *Success Factor Modeling Volume III: Conscious Leadership and Resilience: Orchestrating Innovation and Fitness for the Future,* Dilts Strategy Group 2017 ASIN: B0743M8BR5

For many organizations, *System Leadership* tends to be the most well-understood, and managers jump into its execution by focusing on the ambition and vision regarding what needs to be changed. Key leaders take charge to steer the initiatives through the rough times, often with little balance between work and health and well-being.

But, especially in times of crisis, it is necessary to take the counterintuitive approach of taking the time to share, to develop people, to reflect and to invest in collective team efforts. It is equally important to engage people in more experiential activities where they can express concerns or thoughts using less analytical, verbal modalities and a more metaphorical, visual or somatic approach. More often than not, people are at a loss for words and logic when confronted with a (existential) crisis. If organizations neglect the interpersonal connection of the *Leading-Others-Leadership* and/or the self-care aspects of *Self-Leadership*, many actions taken will be missing aspects of ecology and direction. This typically results in the loss of traction and sustainability within the workforce.

Self-Leadership, in particular, profits from a deep understanding of the *Nine Key Inner Qualities of Good Leaders*. These qualities effectively support any leader or change agent to carry out the four essential actions of Empowering, Coaching, Sharing and Stretching. From an individual perspective ,we can briefly define these actions in the following way:

1. **Passion:** To find what it is that you care deeply about, and for which you have talent, and pursue it with all of your heart. Passion comes from connecting fully with one's self and one's deepest identity and is the foundation for all of the other key qualities of leadership.

2. **Vision:** To set and stay focused on the bigger picture and longer-term goals.

3. **Ambition:** To have "a strong desire to do or to achieve something." Ambition is about directing one's actions towards particular results and maintaining a high level of involvement toward their attainment.

4. **Determination:** To be resolute and firm in one's mission and purpose. Determination fosters the willingness to take risks and try new solutions.

5. **Openness:** To be being curious and available to new ideas. Openness requires having faith in others and building mutual esteem and respect.

6. **Consistency:** To adhere to one's values and beliefs and act ethically and coherently through time. (i.e., "walk the talk").

7. **Motivation:** To be driven to move forward, to "be there," to involve oneself with passion and to invest energy into action.

8. **Generosity:** To dedicate time and personal involvement in order to contribute to the recognition and development of other people's potential. Generosity is the quality of readiness to give more of something, such as time or other resources, than is strictly necessary or expected.

9. **Example:** To provide a believable and trustworthy point of reference—i.e., a model to follow. Being an example has to do with the congruency between "message" and "messenger."

As a generative consultant and change leader that cares for each individual within your or your client's team, recognizing patterns of imbalance or the absence of one or more of these nine qualities in yourself or key stakeholders will raise a red flag which you will either need to address on your own or with human resource representatives. Often, such key individuals can profit from specific and targeted coaching support to stay well and in their top performing state throughout a given crisis situation.

In summary, the visible and measurable actions involved in applying the SFM Leadership Model™ during a crisis are:

* Formulating and communicating a meaningful and inclusive direction for change on all levels.

* Focusing on a higher, longer-term purpose and giving the hope needed.

* Influencing all people involved through inspiration and authenticity.

* Integrating multiple perspectives by involving all team members with respect to the situation at hand.

* Leading by example (walking the talk).

* Exercising mindful self-leadership and reflecting thoughtfully despite stress and pressure

3.7 Strategies to lead change with head and heart

The primary challenge involved in dealing with a crisis is to accelerate the process of change in the right direction. Strategies and tools for dealing effectively with crisis situations include the ability to take distance from the matter at hand and look at it from an "observer" position. By doing so, you will help your clients to avoid getting drawn into negative states and the resulting negative outcomes.

To create a pull towards a positive outcome, maintaining an "outcome frame" and establishing empowering beliefs will help you and your client to move in a generative direction.

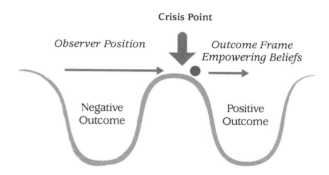

Fig 2. The generative path for surviving crisis

To accomplish this, you as generative consultant need to help your clients to make decisions, communicate their decisions clearly and effectively, and to configure people in order to implement those decisions.

Such leadership activities mainly takes place along the dimensions of (1) carrying out key *tasks* and establishing and (2) strengthening core *relationships*.

* *Making decisions* is primarily focused on the critical path of tasks which need to be carried out.

* *Implementing decisions* tends to be more focused on forming and supporting key relationships—i.e., configuring the people and the organization so that they can successfully complete the tasks which have been decided upon.

* *Communicating decisions* involves a balance of attention with respect to both tasks and relationships. The latter is more often than not the reason why friction occurs in the implementation of decisions. Communication is not targeted or understandable enough for the rest of the workforce that was not involved in the decision making process in the first place.

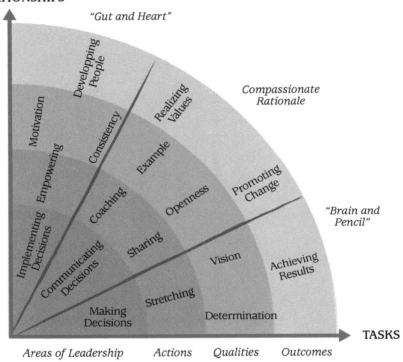

RELATIONSHIPS

"Gut and Heart"

Developping People

Motivation

Consistency

Realizing Values

Empowering

Example

Compassionate Rationale

Implementing Decisions

Coaching

Openness

Promoting Change

"Brain and Pencil"

Communicating Decisions

Sharing

Vision

Achieving Results

Making Decisions

Stretching

Determination

TASKS

Areas of Leadership   *Actions*   *Qualities*   *Outcomes*

Fig 3. Overview of the Leadership with head and heart and its outcomes

Making decisions is fundamentally about the organizational outcome of *achieving results*, and determining the results that are to be the focus of the team and organization. In a crisis situation, this involves a good deal of *stretching*—i.e., getting the most from the (often limited) resources available. The ability to effectively stretch in order to achieve results requires the qualities of *vision*—in order to stay focused on long-term goals and to imagine possible scenarios— and *determination*—in order to follow through with the plan that has been chosen. Making effective decisions is primarily related to what some executives refer to as the "brain and pencil" aspects of leadership.

Communicating decisions is targeted toward the organizational outcomes of both *promoting change* and *realizing values*. Change is necessary in order to be able to adapt to the challenges of the crisis, but core values must be clarified and maintained in order to have a point of reference for stability and coherency. Promoting change requires *sharing* and *openness*, so that key information may be exchanged freely and readily. To realize values, leaders must provide concrete demonstrations of those values through their own *example*, and be prepared to *coach* people in situations where they lack knowledge or experience. The key to maintaining an effective balance between promoting change and realizing values is to have a compassionate rationale for the change.

Implementing decisions effectively is the result of the capacity for *developing people*. The critical leadership action necessary to accomplish this outcome is that of *empowering*—so that people can learn and internalize the basic competencies necessary to effectively accomplish tasks. Effective empowering has to be done by providing objectives and priorities because, as a number of leaders have pointed out, "if you empower without people understanding the environment, they will make the wrong decision." Thus, effectively empowering people requires the leadership qualities of consistency and motivation. *Consistency* is necessary for people to be clear about goals and priorities. *Motivation* is essential to ensure the appropriate investment of energy and action necessary to get the job done.

3.8 Three tools and their generative use in crisis

As referred to in Chapter 1 and earlier in this chapter, one of the key strategies of any generative change agent is to engage multiple intelligences and use not only words but also visual or somatic representations to make sense of a situation. It may feel odd at first for leaders to demonstrate how they perceive a crisis by using a body posture or by using a metaphor. Yet, by embodying the situation physically or transposing it into a metaphor, some solutions will begin to show themselves more readily than by staying limited to verbal logic. Having a leader show the crisis situation with his or her body or by specifying elements using a metaphor, while asking questions like: "What do you need most now? What are you missing now, from you, from your team, from your stakeholders?" will frequently help to more readily get an in-depth situation analysis and some hints for possible next steps than any purely rational discussion of the topic.

a) *Mapping danger & opportunity*

One very useful tool for Facets 1 and 2 in the SFM DIAMOND Model for generative consulting is the mapping of *danger and opportunity*, which is best applied using multiple intelligences. It helps you support your clients or your team not only to explore a crisis situation from a "needs to be fixed" perspective but also to explore and identify certain aspects differently by finding the potential positive consequences (or secondary gains) in the situation. To explain this tool using the "glass half-empty/half-full metaphor, you would ask, "What is the opportunity if the glass is only half-full?" Ideas could be: "There is space to breath. If you empty it, there is less water spilled than in a full glass," or even "You can fill it with something else and get a mixed drink."

Key questions to be explored, include:

1. What is the **danger**?

2. What is the **opportunity**?

3. What is the **decision** that must be made, or "threshold" that must be crossed? What is the unknown territory outside of your comfort zone into which you must step as leader or a team?

4. What is this crisis '**calling**' you to do or become as leader/as team? What is the "call to action?"—If you accepted this calling, who would you become? (It is often useful to answer this question in the form of a symbol or metaphor).

5. What **resources** do you have as leader/team and which do you need to develop more fully in order to effectively address the crisis?

6. Who are (will be) your **supporters** or **guardians** for these resources?

It is important to apply language that accesses multiple intelligences using deepening questions for each step such as: "What do you see? What does it look like for you? How would you describe it using a visual image or a metaphor? Thinking about it, what kind of body sensation do you have?" Possible answers for negative outcomes can include: "a stone in my stomach, speechless, a headache, it feels unstable, heavy."

Engaging the use of multiple intelligences can be extremely rich, especially for the first three questions. It can be particularly helpful to engage the somatic exploration of Question 3 regarding the decision to be made or threshold to be crossed and contrasting it with the dangers and opportunities. You will get much more insightful answers for questions 4-6 if you dare to guide your clients in that way.

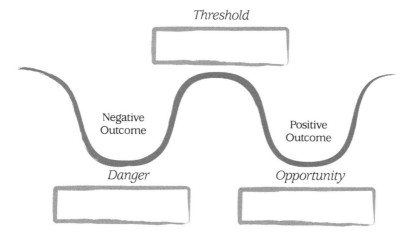

Fig 4. Danger / Opportunity Mapping

b) Building a winning belief system

Effectively dealing with crisis requires the establishment of a "winning belief system." Winning beliefs are directly related to the five fundamental components of the cause-and-effect chain required to achieve change described below.

1. The *outcomes* that the individual, team or organization is trying to achieve.

2. The *path* of steps that leads to those outcomes.

3. The *behaviors* or actions required to successfully travel the path

4. The *plan* specifying the capabilities and qualities needed in order to execute those behaviors and actions effectively.

5. The *people* or team who must possess the capabilities and qualities needed to take the actions and successfully complete the path leading to the desired outcome.

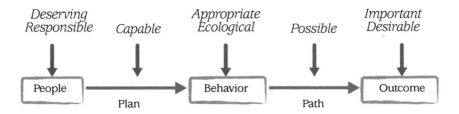

Fig 5. Belief issues related to achieving change

The following checklist will help you to make a *Winning Belief Assessment* for internal as well as external aspects, using the SFM Circle of Success as a guide. This assessment is directly related to the key aspects of the CoS meta mindset, such as Vision (V), Mission (M), Ambition (A) and Role (R). As a word of caution, sometimes people agree and have strong attachments to the vision but struggle with the mission or ambition. This makes it paramount to disclose such differences in order to obtain a valuable assessment. As always, your ability to use inquiring language that points to reflection using all 5 senses as well as aesthetic intelligence in order to seek balance and harmony is key for truly generative insights.

A) **Internally**

    1. In order to get through the current crisis, which belief(s) would be most important for you as leader or a team to strengthen?

        _ The V,M,A are important and worth it.

        _ It is possible to achieve the V,M,A

        _ What I am/we are doing will work to achieve the V,M,A.

        _ I am/we are capable to do what needs to be done to achieve the V,M,A.

        _ I/We deserve to achieve the V,M,A.

2. What inner resource would you need in order to be more congruent or confident regarding the belief(s) that you need to strengthen?

3. Who would be your role model or mentor for that resource?

4. Put yourself into the shoes of your role model or mentor and look at yourself through their eyes (second position). What message or advice would that role model or mentor have for you?

5. Return to your own perspective and review how any insights gained affect you or your team's degree of confidence and congruence.

B) **Externally**

1. In order to get through the current crisis, which belief(s) would be most important for customers, team members, stakeholder or partners to strengthen?

    _ The V,M,A are important and worth it.

    _ It is possible to achieve the V,M,A.

    _ What we are doing will work to achieve the V,M,A.

    _ We are capable to do what needs to be done to achieve the V,M,A.

    _ We deserve to achieve the V,M,A.

2. Who could be a role model to customers, team members, stakeholders or partners for that/those particular belief(s)?

3. What inner resource or message does that role model represent?

4. How does that resource or message affect your team members', stakeholders' or partners' degree of confidence and congruence?

c) The WHAT WILL / WILL NOT HAPPEN Matrix

In many crisis and situations of change, one of my first actions as a change consultant is to distinguish between facts, assumptions and fears. Over the past decade, I have developed a simple Cartesian diagram (see the accompanying figure) that has been most helpful for this process. The first thing to do is to map out a matrix of four boxes. On one axis is what either *will* or *will not happen* with the implementation of the changes that are either assumed or proposed, The other axis identifies what *will happen anyway* and what are the *possible missed opportunities* (i.e., "What will not happen without change" box).

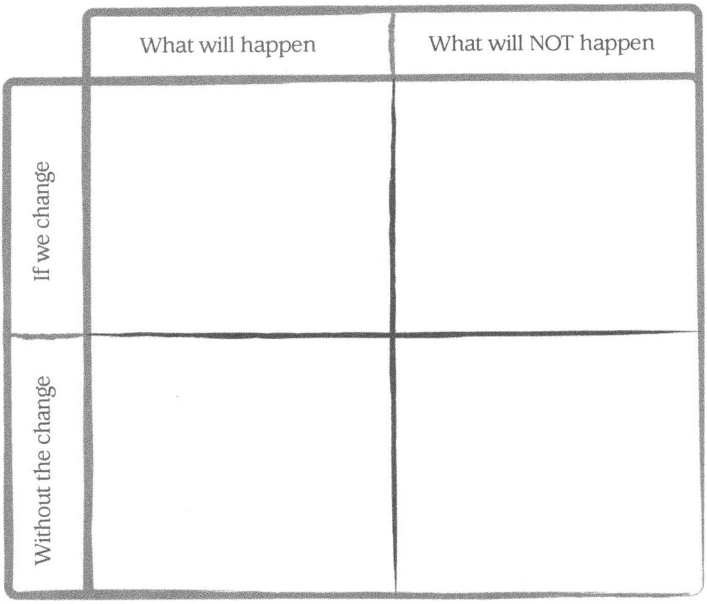

Fig 7. What Will and Will Not Happen Matrix

I use this simple four-box-matrix either in conversation with individuals or as a team exercise to steer meetings held to sort all of the different information and perspectives.

I have also applied it successfully during kick-off events with several hundred people to gain better understanding and insight with respect to counterbalancing arguments and increase the level of understanding and alignment of the workforce.

I have also found it especially useful as a source to craft overall change messages and put them into perspective with respect to one another. Doing so allows leaders and team members to address concerns, fears and hopes with a more balanced perspective. If the various levels of success factors presented in Chapter 1 (environment, behaviors, capabilities, values and beliefs, identity and purpose) are also included, the process becomes a key clarification tool for all stakeholders involved.

From a practical standpoint, there are many ways to work with this matrix. Here are three possibilities:

1. As an open brainstorming tool with you as facilitator. Team members bring up statements and say to which box each belongs.

2. As a structured framework. Client fills in each box in a first round and then review their answers with you as facilitator. You have your clients reflect on their answers and balance them or check, if the answer in box one is true, how can what they have put in the other boxes be true as well.

3. As an independent group exercise. Trams are split into three or four groups that work on one particular box for around five minutes using flipcharts or paper on a table. The teams then rotate to the next flipchart or table and reflect on what the previous groups already collected in that box. It is essential that no one is allowed to cross out any statements but is only allowed to enhance them or ask questions about them. This process is repeated until all groups have worked on each of the four boxes and are back to their original flipchart. Then you invite them to get back into small groups and reflect on what has changed for them, before bringing them back together to reflect and share insights as a whole group.

3.9. A brief case study - Unleashing creative potential in crisis in the FMCG market

In 2009 I started working with several functions at the headquarters of a multinational company in the fast-moving consumer goods (FMCG) industry. The company was facing a rapid decline in sales and an increase in market regulations on multiple levels. The top management contacted me because they were unsatisfied with the cookie-cutter approach used by another consulting firm and were looking for a more customized solution. At first, they considered the very organic approach of the SFM DIAMOND Model that I proposed to be too disruptive, as they wanted quick solutions. But I was able to convince them that they would find more sustainable solutions by attending to what was in the company system (focusing on the first 3 Facets of the SFM DIAMOND Model) rather than dictating solutions.

One particular function was struggling with low trust in management and in the company's capability to adequately respond to the shifting consumer market. The state of the function within the company had basically devolved into a "them vs. us" situation as the market dynamic had started to dramatically decline and competitors had surged ahead in the development of new products. The goal was to build trust, form an aligned vision and unleash the creative potential of that function.

The two key areas on which I worked with the function's management team were to *promote change* and to *develop people*. The focus was placed on Sharing and Empowering by introducing several tools and measures to enhance (1) feedback, (2) unbiased listening and (3) the delegation of decision making to the lowest management level possible. This process started simultaneously with the vice president and the first line managers who all embraced the "we are all in the same boat" perspective. The proposed multilevel change plan included leadership trainings, the improvement of information channels and a shift in how meetings were run.

Leaders and employees began to recognize that they could only be successful together. They were able to establish an integrated vision through a collaborative team effort. Some tools I used to access multiple intelligences included:

* Visual cards to elicit metaphors for their current experience of crisis which allowed us to map issues across several levels of the organization and make links to the SFM Circle of Success.

* Focus groups with 20% of the workforce addressing current and future states with questions such as: "If your team were a car, what brand would it be?" And "Which of your own products or product parts would best describe what you want to achieve?" (This leveraged the employees' strong bond with their product lines.)

* Collage work with the leadership team to visualize their vision and resources in the system.

* Applying the "What will and will not happen" matrix in subteams after the vision was established in order to generate a better understanding and to address rumors.

First results of the multilevel change activities were visible within six months and sustainably grew over a three-year period, resulting in the following hard data from an employee survey:

* The level of trust in management increased by 50 %

* The level of feedback by managers increased by 57 %

* Implementation of good ideas increased by 60 %

* Best practice sharing increased by 33 %

It goes without saying that the impact of a better flow in this function substantially contributed to a boost in innovation. The function spear-headed several new product variations, increased the speed to market and started a totally new product line. Ultimately, the company was able to regain a stellar leadership position in its market segment..

3.10 Key competencies of generative consultants and business leaders during crisis

In times of crisis when everyone is finger pointing, expectations are high to unrealistic and a new way of doing things is often undermined by the need for stability and safety, one of the key competencies as change leader is to make yourself heard and understood. In order for employees to (a) feel able to embrace a new approach, (b) understand what is in it for them and (c) access a certain state of flow, which is needed for achieving excellence, they must feel safe, valued, and vested.

This requires from any leader or consultant a very high level of emotional intelligence, influencing skills and the ability to think and interact systemically. As we established in Chapter 1:

* *Emotional intelligence* – involves the ability to work with emotional states and to detect emotional undercurrents (e.g., the shadow/"elephant in the room" no one is talking about). This is an essential competence for identifying and dealing with obstacles and resistance.

* *Influencing skills* – involve the ability to persuade through presence, congruence and alignment. An effective consultant needs to be able to motivate and influence key people to take action, especially when those actions are unfamiliar and potentially risky.

* *Systemic thinking* – involves the ability to see how things fit into the bigger picture and work with multiple perspectives or truths. This is necessary in order to make sure that the key elements of the organizational holarchy have been considered and addressed. It is particularly important for gathering information and planning actions.

These three competences are also part of the SFM DIAMOND Model and complement the competences we presented in Chapter 2 on Growth. We recommend the following self-reflection questions to help assess your level of competence with respect to these key skill areas for surviving crisis.

a) Emotional intelligence self-reflection questions

1. How did you ensure to seek out and include feelings and emotional responses in your interactions?

2. How well were you able to identify and address any unspoken or hidden feelings or emotional reactions?

3. Did you verbally acknowledge and welcome all of the emotional responses that emerged during your interactions, including difficult feelings?

b) Influencing skills self-reflection questions

1. Were you able to maintain a generative state in yourself and others during the interactions, irrespective of how smooth or challenging they were?

2. How effectively did you seek and respond to the positive intention behind disagreements or resistance?

3. Were you able to reframe disagreements and resistance as valuable insights for a more inclusive solution?

c) Systemic thinking self-reflection questions

1. How many different perceptual positions did you acknowledge and include in your interactions?

2. How frequently did you make reference to and draw attention to the bigger picture and long-term consequences of the issues you were addressing in your interactions?

3. Did you maintain a balance of attention between the individual parts and the whole system during your interactions?

3.11. Key messages for generative consultants

In summary, we believe that the following four points are the most critical for you as business leader or generative consultant in any given crisis situation:

* It is important to distinguish between facts, assumptions and fears and reflect them back to the key actors using direct communication and multiple intelligences..

* Creating a "winning belief system" is the fuel for targeted communication. It reignites morale, especially through the use of inquiring language that encourages reflection based on all five senses as well as aesthetic intelligence.

* A conscious leader not only holds everyone else accountable but him/herself as well. And that may require some extra coaching support to keep a balance applying all *Nine Key Inner Qualities of Good Leaders*

* Mastering emotional intelligence is key to stay alert and open to unexpected challenges

To finish on a personal note: to be a generative consultant or leader also means to be a genuine human being with high integrity. Additionally, in crisis situations, you need to be able to hold your ground, embody the vision of what others do not yet see and engage multiple intelligences. This is because many clients or team members will be in the A (Analysis paralysis) mode of the CRASH state. This will sometimes require you to be counterintuitive and bold in choosing your questions, while sailing the rough seas with your client or team in the same boat. Having the nine generative consulting competences and the nine key inner leadership qualities "in your muscles," allows you to draw upon them in any situation and be a present, resourceful co-pilot for any group or organization that needs a beacon or a spark of hope.

"Life is a Journey from Self to Self, passing through so many Others, in a perpetual and ascending movement"

— Unknown author

Chapter 4
How to best manage Transition in Business

Elisabeth Falcone and Jean-François Thiriet

4.1 Overview

In this chapter we focus on how you as a generative consultant or business leader, can utilize the key areas of the SFM Circle of Success™ in situations of transition in order to enhance performance, create new solutions, bring out new ideas and make wiser decisions. We also establish that managing transitions requires organizations to have a proactive approach to change. In doing so, we will detail how generativity requires collective intelligence and share with you the SFM Collective Intelligence Model. Lastly, we will further explore why communication, presentation and facilitation skills are key for successfully managing transition.

4.2 Why is this chapter important?

The skills and tools presented in this chapter will boost your ability as a generative consultant and change leader to generate powerful discussions with as many stakeholders in the system as possible. This is important since exploring the depth and scope of the holon is key in situations of transition. We will provide an example of how we helped one of our clients unlock their capacity for collective intelligence using the PERICEO™ tool and how that supported the awakening of their collective IQ and wisdom.

4.3 Setting the context: What is transition? And what is collective intelligence?

It is a fact that everything changes all the time. Everything that is alive is in constant flux. Life has cycles; therefore every living being is always transitioning from one stage to another. You, me, organizations, and economic, sociological and political systems are all living organisms. It is even all the more true these days in the corporate world. We call this "VUCA[1]" (as briefly discussed in the introduction to the previous chapter), which means: volatile, uncertain, complex and ambiguous:

* Volatile, because of the inconstancy of situations faced by business leaders.

* Uncertainty, about situations that cannot be predicted and results that are not guaranteed, which forces business leaders to be more responsive and change their management methods.

---

1   https://en.wikipedia.org/wiki/Volatility,_uncertainty,_complexity_and_ambiguity

* Complexity, in relation to the growing number of interactions within the organization's ecosystem and market sector of activity, which compels them to highlight the skills of each employee, and to capitalize on decision-making that involves each of them.

* Ambiguity, with regard to the challenge of distinguishing between cause-and-effect relationships and difficulties in reading regulations – either legal or normative, which forces business leaders to develop their intuition in addition to their cognitive abilities instead of relying on their past achievements and their certainties.

The question then is:"Will these transitions take the form of vicious circles – a chain of mechanisms that create and sustain adverse effects – or rather virtuous ones – a set of causes and effects that improve the entire system?" In this context, collective intelligence takes on its full meaning because, as we have mentioned, one person can no longer have the ability to understand all the issues. We define collective intelligence as *the ability of people in a team, a group, or an organization to share knowledge, think, and act in an aligned and coordinated fashion to achieve critical results.*

Importance of the transition phase

According to William Bridges[2], most organizations seem to go through some type of archetypal journey:

* ***"Once upon a time":*** The founder starts to dream the dream, and the vision is put into words.

* ***"Then one day":*** He or she gives birth to the venture. At this stage the way of moving forward is "making it up as we go."

* ***"Because of this":*** The venture needs to get organized: structure, processes, roles, and policies are spelled and put into action.

* ***The climax:*** At this stage, the venture becomes stable enough to become an institution. It stops fighting for new markets, and has arrived. Its priority is more about keeping what has been achieved and less about moving forward. The connection between the venture and its environment loosens. The focus is more inward than outward.

---

2   William Bridges, *Managing Transitions*, 2003, Perseus Publishing

* ***If nothing is done, the dying of the hero:*** If nothing is set in motion, if growth is not sufficiently discussed, and if bureaucracy takes over, then the venture goes bankrupt or disappears because of the obsolescence of its product, structure or processes.

* ***Or the rise of the hero:*** When a relatively established venture prepares for inner and outer changes.

The moral of the tale: Organizations need to manage transition, which is at the core of proactive change or transformation management.

Reactive or proactive change management ?

Transition can be defined as a state of major adjustment that occurs when relatively established ventures prepare for inner and outer adaptations to cope with ongoing growth and change. As the archetypal journey cited above indicates, transition is frequently initiated in a stable economy and mature market and reflects a planned and conscious approach to being ready to successfully master the future. This is in contrast to abrupt changes precipitated by crisis, as described in the previous chapter. Even though transition is an ever-happening process, we will treat it in this chapter as a specific stage in the life of a venture.

Issues and challenges met during transition

Change typically takes place at a physical level, in the environment for instance, whereas effective transition relates to adaptations in the psychological and cultural dimensions of an organization. Be aware that change is inevitable, whereas effective transition may not be. Keeping in mind the SFM Model of Mindset, Actions and Outcomes (see page 22) as a generative consultant and change leader, you will want to go beyond applying physical or behavioral change tools and address the mindset aspects of transition. Reactive change measures are more related to surviving crisis (covered in the previous chapter). Managing transition requires proactive efforts.

The purpose of managing transition is precisely to avoid crisis by anticipating and preparing for possible major disruptions, such as a significant shift in the economy or market, or the retirement of key executives. Transition can also be precipitated following a time of crisis. In this case, you as a generative consultant will want to help the members of an organization become more proactive with regard to the next step in their evolution. This involves helping them to move beyond their comfort zone and address (1) their possible resistance to reorganizing or (2) their existing complacency and inertia.

"If it is not broken, don't fix it".

- Common Saying

In an organizational system where there is little motivation to embrace change, a common attitude is, "If it's not broken, don't fix it." In such a context, there is a greater risk for low to no innovation.

Further, because future conditions can be difficult to predict, the desired state of the transition may not yet have taken shape, and people may not even be clear about what or where the destination is. In this case, the only certainty is that you have left behind the way things used to be, but you haven't yet arrived at a new point of stability. Under these conditions, people typically seek safety and security in what is familiar.

Managing times of transition requires building motivation by reconnecting to the passion, mission and legacy at the heart of the venture. It also involves developing greater ability to detect weak signals and to anticipate and communicate trends. In order to progress through times of transition, it is important to cultivate qualities such as flexibility, balance, confidence, connection and the ability to let go. When people and organizations have the necessary mindset, tools, resources and roadmaps for this journey, they eventually arrive at a place of greater wholeness which both includes and transcends their previous states.

Vital elements to investigate while managing transition – The S.C.O.R.E. model

As you are well aware by now, the S.C.O.R.E. model is a great tool to use in the first steps of the SFM DIAMOND model for generative consulting. It helps you to identify the key elements involved in managing an organization's transition such as those listed in the following table:

Managing Transition

Symptoms	Possible Causes		Desired Outcomes	Possible Resources	Effects
	Outer	**Inner**			
• What used to work does not work anymore. No significant action. • Retardation. • Complacency • Malaise • Inertia • Staying within the comfort zone • Low to no innovation • "We have always done it this way" • "Just because things have changed does not mean that anything's different around here" mindset.	• Stable economy • Mature/ Saturated market • Established in life cycle. • Growing competition • Fast technology evolution • New laws • "Uberisation" (commoditizing) products or services	• No Passion, • No Vision • No Ambition • Focus only on strong signals. • Stuck in realist state. • Fixed Identity namely on its "status" • Avoiding Chaos • Fear Of volatility • Conflicts between generations • Challenge with letting go of what has worked	• Ensure quick success • Define what needs to change and what does not. • Prepare for inner or outer changes • Optimize structures and processes. • Targeted incremental innovation • Symbolize the new identity.	• Reconnect to mission and legacy. • Detect weak signals, • Anticipate and communicate trends. • Treat the past with respect, insist on what continues.	• The system starts moving again. • "Life" reappears. • An alignment to a new direction appears. • Innovations emerge, different ways of being and doing. • People begin to pay attention to weak signals and learn to take advantage of "chaos".

As we have pointed out earlier, effective transition is not inevitable in times of change. You may recognize some of the company names below as they are infamous for being unable to adapt and make the transition from symptoms to outcomes:

* **Kodak**: A major tech company in the photographic film market in the 90's which was not able to adapt to the digital age because of the impact of digital cameras on the film market. They filed for bankruptcy in 2012.

* **Nokia**: The first company to create a cellular network and became the global leader in mobile phones. They overlooked that Internet and data would be the future of mobile phones and lost the game in 2008.

* **MySpace:** The leader in social media early 2000. At one point, Mark Zuckerberg even offered to sell Facebook to MySpace for 75 million dollars. They finally lost so many users that they had to fire 500 employees in 2011, six years later.

And the list goes on: IBM, Blackberry, Segway, Hitachi, Xerox, Toshiba, Motorola, Palm (remember these ones?!), Atari and Hummer. It will be interesting to see how Twitter, Uber, Victoria's Secret and others will manage the curve.[3]

Other useful frameworks for identifying key factors to manage transition

As we stipulate in our SFM DIAMOND model for generative change, the more perspectives you have on an issue the more options you get to resolve it. It is valuable to apply this principle to help your client or team explore their own context, in order to generate the motivation to change. Even if VUCA has become the norm, being able to help your clients to read the field to which they belong is key in transition.

The PESTLE framework

A useful structure to help with the information gathering phase of the DIAMOND Model is the PESTLE framework[4] which supports clients and team members to identify potential threats and opportunities. PESTLE stands for:

---

3   https://valuer.ai/blog/the-next-big-companies-to-fail-in-5-10-years/)

4   https://pestleanalysis.com/what-is-pestle-analysis/

* **Political**: Government policies, political stability, foreign trade policy, tax policy, etc.

* **Economic**: Macro or micro economic factors – economic growth, interest rates, inflation, disposable incomes of consumers, etc.

* **Social**: Values and beliefs shared by customers and their sense of culture, age distribution, health consciousness, etc.

* **Technological**: New trends in production, distribution, communication, etc.

* **Legal**: Consumer rights, advertising standards, etc.

* **Environmental**: Scarcity of raw material, ethical stakes, carbon footprint, etc.

The underlying idea is to build traction among the different stakeholders of the organization by helping them to create a bigger picture of the system to which they belong. To do so, gather the key stakeholders in the same place at the same time and assign each of them a part of the PESTLE puzzle so that a pertinent SWOT (Strengths, Weaknesses, Opportunities, Threats) or SOAR (Strength, Opportunities, Aspirations, Results) analysis can emerge. You can even facilitate this tool with learning journeys to observe the field in person and by doing so help the members of the organization to open their eyes to the reality of their environment.

The PERICEO™ Tool

In the same way that the PESTLE framework addresses the outside of an organization's system, the PERICEO™ assessment tool creates a link with an organization's inner workings. It was developed to assess an organizations degree of collaborative ability and *collective intelligence*. Applying the *Key Levels of Success Factors* described in Chapter 1, the PERICEO assessment tool creates the opportunity to promote an in-depth and necessary discussion among an organization's key stakeholders encouraging a number of different perspectives. It can be used as diagnostic tool or as a framework to moderate discussions.

Especially in times of transition within organizations, a deep level of engagement in conversations is a key success factor for transition to occur with the best possible odds.

The PERICEO tool applies a series of scorecards to be filled in by the relevant members of the team or group involved in the assessment process. Each scorecard is focused on one of the Key Levels of Success Factors (i.e., vision and purpose, identity, values and beliefs, capabilities, behaviors, environment) necessary for successfully managing transition. The scorecards present several dimensions of each success factor to be rated on a scale from 1 to 5, with "1" representing the most degenerative state of that factor and "5" representing its most generative state.

As a generative consultant/facilitator you can distribute the scorecards to the group you are facilitating, making sure that each member answers individually first. This is a necessary condition for collective intelligence to occur and a good way to prevent people from getting lost in "groupthink." Once people have individually filled in their scorecards, they can share their different answers and perspectives with one another. It is amazing to see how differences in perception are starters for really insightful talks that support the first step of the SFM DIAMOND Model.

Key Factors for Vision

Success Factor	Low Level	1+1= -1	1+1= 0	1+1= 1	1+1= 2	1+1= 3	High Level
1. The Vision is Ecological for the system, the individuals and the collective.	The vision ignores either the individual or the collective or both..	1	2	3	4	5	The Vision is constantly serving individuals AND the collective.
2. The Vision inspires action, commitment and self-improvement.	No commitment or self-initiative.	1	2	3	4	5	Numerous and spontaneous actions and commitments.
3. The Vision provides a clear direction.	There is no obvious sense of direction.	1	2	3	4	5	The direction is clear and known by all.
4. The Vision inspires innovation.	No innovation.	1	2	3	4	5	Numerous and regular innovations.
5. The Vision unites people.	People think and act as individuals.	1	2	3	4	5	Team members share a strong sense of connection and common purpose.

Example SCORECARD: Key Factors for Vision

"Radar" representation (with an example) :

Key Factors of Vision

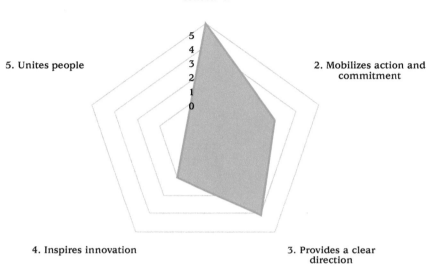

1. Serves both the individual and the collective.

5. Unites people

2. Mobilizes action and commitment

4. Inspires innovation

3. Provides a clear direction

Results from the scorecards can be represented in different ways. The figure above shows an example of a scorecard and a corresponding "radar" chart for a team member's rating of the organization's vision. This gives us a very clear visual representation of the current state of that success factor and shows the areas for improvement.

Ratings for a particular level of success factors are synthesized and a summary is provided of the state of that factor in the team, group or organization. For example, the following table summarizes the different levels of maturity with regard to an organization's vision.

Success Factor	1 Low Level $1 + 1 = -1$	2 $1 + 1 = 0$	3 $1 + 1 = 1$	4 $1 + 1 = 2$	5 High Level $1 + 1 = 3$
Vision	In your organization the vision is of a level $1 + 1 = -1$, which means that for the most part for people it is rather degenerative. This can mean for example that the vision ignores either the individual or the collective or both, or there is no commitment or self-initiative, or no obvious, shared sense of direction. It can also mean that there's no innovation, or that people think and act as separate individuals. It is also possible that many of these reasons are cumulative.	In your organization the vision is of a level $1 + 1 = 0$, which means that for the most part for people it is rather null. This can mean for example that the vision begins to take into account the individual or the collective, or that a few commitment or self-initiative appear, or that sometimes the direction is shared or known by people. This can also mean that there are some few rare and unpredictable innovations, or that sometimes people feel connected around the Vision. It is also possible that many of these reasons are cumulative.	In your organization the vision is of a level $1 + 1 = 1$, which means that for the most part for people it's like there's only one person. This can mean for example that sometimes the vision is at the service of the individual or the collective, or that we can find some commitments and scattered initiatives. This can also be the case where the direction is known by only a few people, or we can find more unpredictable innovations, or some people connect around the Vision. It is also possible that many of these reasons are cumulative.	In your organization the vision is of a level $1 + 1 = 2$, which means for the most part for people it's actually collected intelligence. This can mean for example that the Vision is serving the individual and the collective but not constantly, or that we find more and more commitments and initiatives, or that more and more people know and share the Vision. This can also be that there are some regular innovations, and that more and more people feel connected around the Vision. It is also possible that many of these reasons are cumulative.	In your organization the vision is of a level $1 + 1 = 3$, which is exactly the level of collective Intelligence. This means that for the most part for people the vision is constantly serving individuals AND the collective, and that there are numerous and spontaneous actions and commitments. The direction is clear and known by all, there are numerous and regular innovations. Team members share a strong sense of connection and common purpose.

The PERICEO tool generates a report, presenting results and suggesting tools and processes for improvement.

The following example shows a summary of all of the Key Levels of Success Factors – from Vision to Environment. This gives a global view of the overall state of collective intelligence in the team, group or organization.

GLOBAL SUMMARY

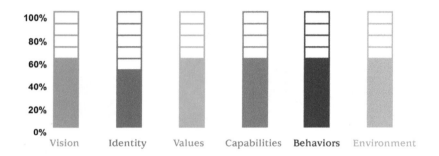

Global Results

* **Vision:** 61.26% More than moderately developed but still needs further attention.

* **Identity:** 53.16% Moderately developed but needs further attention.

* **Values:** 57.89% More than moderately developed but still needs further attention.

* **Capabilities:** 57.89% More than moderately developed but still needs further attention.

* **Behaviors:** 58.3% More than moderately developed but still needs further attention.

* **Environment:** 59.47% More than moderately developed but still needs further attention.

Extract from a report relating to a national private group in France. Study carried out with the Board of Directors.

Global results can be broken down into the specific ratings of the individuals involved in the assessment process. The individual ratings can be compared (as in the following example graphs) in order to acknowledge different perspectives and promote exchanges between participants in the assessment. These exchanges can improve the level of collective intelligence and support the search for innovative solutions.

Individual Results for Vision

1. The Vision is Ecological for the system, the individuals and the collective.

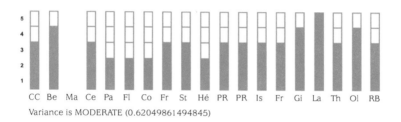

Variance is MODERATE (0.62049861494845)

2. The Vision inspires action, commitment and self-improvement.

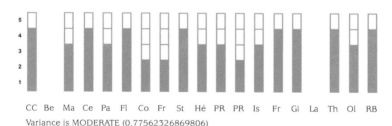

Variance is MODERATE (0.77562326869806)

3. The Vision provides a clear direction.

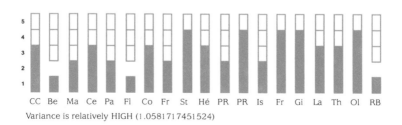

Variance is relatively HIGH (1.0581717451524)

The PERICEO tool can be used on a large scale to gather and synthesize a diversity of perspectives or on a team-by-team basis (marketing team, manufacturing team, design team, finance team, human resources team, etc.) in order to create an individual team profile. The whole idea is to create a space for all the relevant parts of the organizational "holon" to become involved in the discussion.

Once areas for improvement are identified, the PERICEO tool suggests possible causes and recommends "improvement tracks."

Team Results for Vision

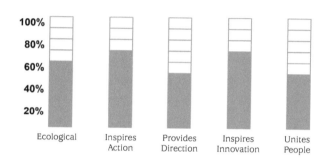

1. The Vision is Ecological for the system, the individuals and the collective.

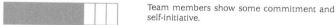

The Vision sometimes ignores the individual or the collective.

POSSIBLE CAUSE: A reflection has begun to be conducted and communicated, but the work that has been made on the vision needs to be adjusted for both individuals and the collective.

IMPROVEMENT TRACK: Work on the Vision and how to make it happen in every department every team in the organization. CATALYST: Work on Resonance-Synergy-Emergence. Work with VMAR. Communicate on the Vision.

2. The Vision inspires action, commitment and self-improvement.

Team members show some commitment and self-initiative.

POSSIBLE CAUSE: The vision is poorly communicated and known to few stakeholders, or few collaborators are aligned with it. .

IMPROVEMENT TRACK: Work and communicate on the Vision at all levels of the organization, in all teams. CATALYST: COACH state - InterVision.

For more information about this tool, see *The PERICEO Tool: Teams and Organizations Increase Your Capacity for Collective Intelligence* (2018) or go to the PERICEO website: www.periceo.com.

The Co-Alignment Process

A good example of implementing an improvement track is the SFM Co-Alignment Process. The top managers of every major organization are no doubt familiar with the concepts of vision, mission and ambition. It can be a powerful experience for them, however, to literally move from vision to action. This is what the Co-Alignment Process can help to accomplish. It creates the conditions for a structured discussion among key actors and helps them to include all the steps needed to achieve success.

To facilitate this process, you will want to create six locations in a line on the floor. One spot for vision and purpose, another for identity and mission, then values and beliefs, capabilities, behaviors and environment. You next invite all members of the team or group to stand next to each other and physically walk along this line while having them explore the following questions:

* *What is the vision we are pursuing as a team or organization?*

* *What is our desired identity and mission in relationship to that vision and the clients we are serving?*

* *What are the core values and beliefs necessary to support that mission?*

* *What are the key capabilities necessary to implement the mission and core values?*

* *What portfolio of activities expresses and manifests our mission and values?*

* *What are the significant environments or contexts in which we desire to operate?*

At each step of the way, key actors are to answer the question for themselves first (beware of groupthink rather than collective alignment) and, afterwards, share their answers with the group.

4.4 Supporting transition in a generative way

Referring back to the organizational archetypal journey introduced at the beginning of this chapter, you as a generative consultant will want to help your clients avoid the "dying of the hero" pitfall. You can do this by inspiring them to move towards a "proactive" versus a "reactive" approach to change, in order to "be ahead of the curve."

A good metaphor to share with your clients is that of frogs versus bats. Frogs and bats have the same food source – flying insects. But they have completely different strategies for catching their prey. Basically, frogs are "reactive" and sit on lily pads waiting for the food to come to them, whereas bats are "proactive" and use a very sophisticated sonar system, which is extremely sensitive to weak signals. The difference here is between "waiting for what is coming next" and "looking for what is coming."

It is significant to note that frogs have a life expectancy of two to five years, whereas bats have an average life span of 25 to 40 years. This illustrates the impact of these two strategies on longevity. A proactive attention to weak signals is essential for sustainable success and survival. And this is exactly what you, as a generative consultant or business leader want to help your clients and teams to achieve.

How? By relying on the collective intelligence of the organization. In the dynamic and uncertain stage of transition, establishing key relationships is an important success factor. So, as a generative consultant and change agent, you want to be able to help the organization to stay alive and connected with all its parts: clients, teams, partners, stakeholders, etc. And this is where the SFM Collective Intelligence Model gives us direction.

The SFM Collective Intelligence Model

At the core of what is at stake for a stable organization in transition is the need to create a space to "dream a new dream" (Step 2 of the SFM DIAMOND Model) – to let go of the old to open to the new and move through the insecurity of the neutral zone where people do not know yet what the future will be like.

As we presented in chapter 2, the five key outcomes defined by the SFM Circle of Success are:

1. Personal Satisfaction

2. Financial Robustness and Profitability

3. Scalable Growth

4. Innovation and Resilience

5. Meaningful Contribution

To achieve these outcomes, the SFM Collective Intelligence Model provides four powerful strategies:

1. Enhancing existing performance

2. Creating new solutions (for existing and/or new markets)

3. Fostering new ideas

4. Making wiser decisions

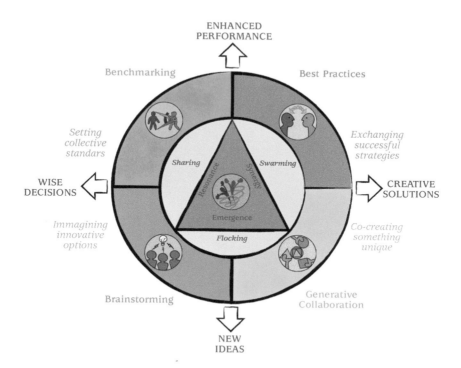

The SFM Collective Intelligence Model: as published in *SFM Volume II – Generative Collaboration: Releasing the Creative Power of Collective Intelligence*

Even if most of your clients or teams will want to achieve every one of these outcomes (who would not?), you will want to bring attention to the main outcome that they want to achieve during their transition, keeping in mind that each of these outcomes will have an impact on every other one.

Actions to encourage

In order to achieve these results, you can encourage the groups with whom you are working to engage in the following actions:

* **Benchmark the market** in order to affirm or set new collective standards;

* **Look for best practices** in their ecosystem and allow sharing of successful strategies;

* **Brainstorm** to come up with innovative options;

* **Open spaces for generative collaboration** where the organization and its system can co-create something unique and disruptive.

And this is exactly where, to support these actions, you need to set up rituals, ways of being and doing, which will facilitate resonance, to highlight synergy and trigger emergence.

Resonance, Synergy and Emergence

Resonance has to do with the questions "Where do we meet?" and "How are we the same?" If we do not perceive connection with each other, we are afraid and we retract. "The other" becomes a stranger. Once we have highlighted areas of resonance, we will want to see where we complement each other.

Synergy comes from exploring the questions "Where are our differences?" and "How can they complement and enrich each other?" This leads to the possibility for something greater than our individual competences to be expressed.

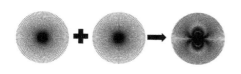

Emergence results from asking, "What else becomes possible through our interaction that is larger than us as individuals?" and "What new can come through our interaction?" This is where the "magic" happens!

Resonance, synergy and emergence are the three pillars of collective intelligence. It is necessary to take the time – and in no case "waste time" – to build these pillars in any group or team process.

Engaging multiple intelligences (visual, somatic, metaphoric, etc.) when establishing such activities will also help your client or team to increase their degree of comprehensiveness and creativity. And, as mentioned before, it is important to encourage participants to find their own responses before sharing with the group in order to avoid "groupthink" and promote truly "collective" intelligence.

4.5 Facilitation skills and knowledge for a generative consultant

Facilitation Skills

To orchestrate these four actions (benchmarking, sharing best practices, brainstorming and generative collaboration) successfully, you must have strong facilitation skills and knowledge of group dynamics. For instance, you need to know that each step of a collective project (like managing transition) will require some **sharing** of information and ideas so that people in the organization can find the degree of resonance necessary to spark the motivation and aspiration for change. You will also need to be able to direct multiple perspectives and knowhow toward the new dream (**swarming**), and its challenges, which will create synergies between skills and stakeholders. And finally, you will want to help people **flock** in the service of a common purpose, giving birth to the possibility for the emergence of something new.

In order to achieve these results, you can also apply the insights from Google's Aristotle Project – a tribute to the philosopher's famous quote: "The whole is greater than the sum of its parts." They showed[1] that the conditions necessary for teams to develop their Collective IQ are:

---

1   https://rework.withgoogle.com/print/guides/5721312655835136/

* **Equality in distribution of conversational turn-taking:** People talk in the same amount of time to maintain a higher level of collective intelligence. This can be supported by: clear timing around agenda items, using a talking stick, or inviting people into the conversation who are not participating.

* **Social sensitivity:** Attention to non-verbal cues among participants, especially cues relating to emotional states. This is supported by processes like the "meteo" tool, which involves asking participants to share 2 words describing their inner state at the beginning of a work session.

* **Psychological safety:** People are able to share what they genuinely think and feel, and can reveal intimate information about themselves without fear of rejection or punishment. Setting basic behavioral ground rules is usually key here – i.e., what could be called behavioral etiquette. (See the mindset qualities below as a possible map.)

* **Perceived task significance:** People connect their own work to a larger purpose beyond the particular team or organization. This can be supported by taking or making time to share the big "WHY" over and over again so that the people involved in the transition can really own the process.

Establish a supportive mindset between participants

All of these observable behavioral factors also reveal the underlying qualities of mindset that you will want to foster among the teams you facilitate:

* Equality in distribution of conversational turn-taking reflects a mindset of **respect** for one another and **responsibility** for one's own actions

* Social sensitivity comes from a underlying attitude of **caring** and **interest** for others in the group

* Psychological safety reflects a capacity for mutual **trust** and **acceptance**

* Perceived task significance involves a deeper desire for **meaning** through **contribution** to a larger purpose

Be an example: "Walk your talk" with the COACH state Taï Chi

The COACH State Taï Chi involves anchoring the different aspects of the COACH state with both words and somatic movements or gestures.

As a generative consultant and business leader, you will want to embody as fully as possible these qualities of mindset that support collective intelligence – *respect, responsibility, interest, caring, trust, acceptance* and *contribution* – when facilitating your clients and teams. As former Hanover Insurance CEO Bill O'Brien pointed out, "The success of an intervention depends on the interior condition of the intervener."

In Chapter 1 we emphasized the importance of what we called the COACH state in yourself, your clients and your teams. The COACH state, in combination with the use of multiple intelligences, is the foundation for the generative state, which is essential for any type of generative change. Thus, fostering this state in yourself and your clients is an important ongoing practice.

A good way to integrate the practice of COACH state with multiple intelligences is what we call the "COACH state Taï Chi." It involves anchoring the various aspects of the COACH state with both words and somatic movements or gestures. You can use the following table as a guide:

Intention: Becoming More	Linguistic Intelligence/mental mantras	Somatic Intelligence
Centered	"I am present." "I am centered."	What movement comes to you?
Open	"I am Open."	Let that movement come to you.
Alert	"I am Aware, I am Awake, Alert and Clear, through my senses."	Let this movement come through you.
Connected	"I am connected to myself, to you, to the field of resources within and around us."	What gesture comes?
Holding / Welcoming	"I am ready to welcome and hold whatever emerges."	Let your body speak.

Make sure that your COACH state is at a level of at least 7 or above on a scale from 0 to 10. Ideally, all the stakeholders involved in the transition would be in a generative state for optimum efficiency.

As you help the organization to move into action while managing transition (Step 4 of the SFM DIAMOND Model), you will want to be sure that the people are in some type of generative state. You may not call it COACH state as such, but keep in mind that the generative state is key to creating effective and sustainable solutions. As we pointed out in Chapter 1, people perceive their reality through their filters; and if their filters are rigid and fixed it means that the reality of the organization will be rigid and fixed as well. Bringing the perceptual filters of the key actors in the transition process into a generative mode is one of your main goals as a generative coach and business leader. This will be primarily supported by three of our key generative consulting competences.

The three main competencies of a generative consultant for managing transition

To help your clients and teams activate their collective intelligence and manage transition, you, as a generative consultant and business leader, have to apply a high level of competence in communication, presentation and facilitation. Again, change is inevitable and is more outwardly oriented, whereas transition is more of a psychological process. Hence, your ability to elicit and orchestrate the exchange of information, insights and actions is a key success factor in managing transition.

As in the previous chapters, we invite you to reflect more deeply on your own level of competence with regard to these skills so you can more clearly identify your areas of strength and areas for improvement. The following self-reflection questions can also be shared with the individuals and teams you work with, since these skills are also needed by the executives and other key actors who need to be active in managing transition.

a) Communication skills

 If you want to help your clients and teams manage transition, you will need to develop or reinforce your communication skills. In generative consulting, this means your fluency in talking to different types and levels of people.

Questions:

1. *Did you adapt your communication approach to reach all types and levels of people involved in the interaction you facilitated?*

2. *How much did you use non-verbal as well as verbal communication during your interactions?*

3. *How quickly were able to perceive and respond to both verbal and non-verbal feedback?*

4. *How often did you use verbal reframing to introduce new perspectives to the situations being discussed?*

b) Presentation skills

Presentation skills involve your ability to speak with an audience using multiple communication channels (verbal, visual, metaphorical, somatic, etc.). The more modalities you use to share a message the more it will be understood and remembered.

Questions:

1. *How clear and helpful was your use of verbal language?*

2. *Did you use images to support a clearer and better understanding of your message?*

3. *Did you use metaphors to help to deepen the understanding of your message?*

4. *How often did you use gestures and other somatic expressions to help keep your audience's attention and promote a better understanding of your message?*

c) Facilitation skills

Once you have helped your client communicate within the organization, and ideally its ecosystem, and you have helped them present the transition in multiple ways, it is time to exercise your ability to facilitate the key dynamics of collective intelligence and promote resonance, synergy and emergence among members of the groups engaged in the transition.

Questions:

1. How frequently did you draw attention to the shared purpose of the group during interactions?

2. How often and in how many different areas did you seek and point out similarities among group members?

3. Did differences between group members create conflict and confusion or were you able to guide the group to explore how their differences complement one another in service of their shared purpose?

4. How much time, space and encouragement did you give for something new and unexpected to arise out of the group interactions?

4.6 Case study applying some of the tools we have presented in this chapter

Applying the PERICEO Team Profile

The PERICEO tool supports two complementary and inseparable approaches to managing transition.

The first one, and the most relevant in our opinion, is to highlight and compare each participant's perceptions of the collective IQ, or level of collective intelligence, with respect to the teams involved. This approach facilitates generative exchanges that increase the team members' awareness of their own processes, which can unlock stuck situations.

The second one is to determine an "average" perception of the level of collective IQ within the teams in order to establish an overall baseline. This approach makes it possible to highlight the general trend of the level of collective intelligence within the organization as a whole.

The PERICEO tool combines these two approaches to managing transitions, with the analysis of the possible causes and improvement tracks, which the generative consultant can refine during his or her exchanges with the teams and management they are supporting.

We propose the following synthetic representation for the overall implementation process.

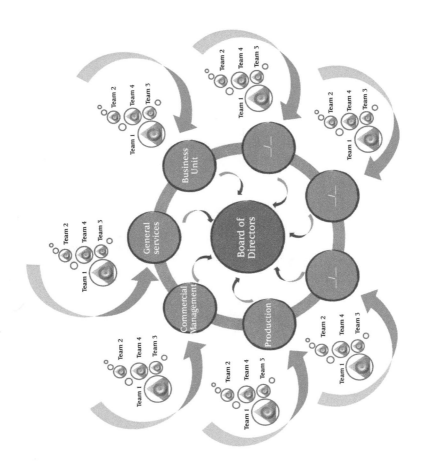

Systemic representation using the PERICEO Team Profile

The following is a case example of how this overall implementation process was applied to help the Food, Agriculture and Forestry Commission of French Guyana manage a major transition. A decentralized service of the Ministry of Agriculture and Forestry, the commission was created in 2011 from a fusion of agriculture, forestry and veterinary services. It was organized into several entities: general secretariat, statistical information systems and economic, strategic management, territorial planning, training and development.

Applying the SFM DIAMOND Model

Applying the seven steps of the SFM DIAMOND Model and building on the nine key competencies, after several months of exchanges, meetings and investigations with the relevant team members, we were able to achieve the following:

1. **D**efining Present State: This organization was mainly in a **transitional situation**, where the management of different services had been merged for the purpose of restructuring. The result was a loss of identity and meaning, no common vision, demotivation, lack of communication and connections, etc. Moreover, the larger context was one of social conflict in a territory whose wealth (Guyanese gold) was coveted and at the same time suffered great poverty.

2. **I**ntention Setting: In this context, the **desired state** of the new management was to work better together, improve collective performance, and change the organization's strategy for contributing to the development of the territory and the well-being of the people who worked there.

3. **A**ction Planning: **Several actions** were identified. The first was to formulate a vision at the CODIR (management committee) level. Another action was to listen to the various stakeholders – including the different partners – in order to identify key needs and to involve all of the collaborators.

4. **M**oving into Action: Different processes of collective intelligence were applied to support movement into action. For example, an Open Space intervention was employed to help define priority actions and create a storyboard for the transition process. The actions and storyboard that emerged enabled groups to apply tools and strategies of collective intelligence to their project management work over the following year. This made it possible to create different working conditions which sparked joy and enthusiasm among all the employees. This, in turn, infused them with a strong desire to participate, thus fulfilling the desired state of performance defined in Step 2.

5. **O**bstacle Transformation: Similarly, collective intelligence and group sponsorship processes made it possible to increase communication, connection and cohesion among teams and to diffuse reactivity and tension between employees due to social conflicts and the fact that employees were scattered throughout the territory.

6. **N**oting Progress: A few months into the intervention, the PERICEO tool was applied in order to evaluate progress and make necessary adjustments. The application of the PERICEO tool confirmed that certain key factors related to the behaviors and the interactions between key collaborators had changed in a positive and observable way.

7. **D**eepening Practices: We helped the organization and the teams to establish practices to support and deepen the changes that took place: practicing the COACH state, intervision groups, the development of SCORECARDS with key success factors, "delegated meetings," a shared collaborative space, a "guardian" system with respect to commitments, generative MasterMind group processes, celebrations, etc.

Making a link with the SFM Circle of Success, this intervention mainly enabled our Guyanese clients to "dream a new dream" and get moving again by adopting a new mindset. Everything that was done followed the four strategies defined by the SFM Collective Intelligence Model listed earlier:

1. Enhance existing performance

2. Create new solutions

3. Foster new ideas

4. Make wiser decisions

These strategies supported them through their transition phase in the best possible conditions.

Applying the S.C.O.R.E. Model

Making a link with the S.C.O.R.E. Model, we can also summarize the situation in the following way:

1. **Symptoms:** Demotivation, lack of communication and connections, tension between employees, lack of team cohesion.

2. **Causes:** Social conflicts throughout the territory and also internally among employees. Claims on the territory (wealth). Paradigm shift and restructuring of state services. No common vision. No passion or ambition. Employees scattered throughout the territory. A state of reactivity in response to context and urgency.

3. **Outcomes:** Identify strategic priorities. Stimulate collective performance. Create different working conditions. Spark and spread joy and enthusiasm. Connect people who would not otherwise meet. Increase employees' awareness of their operating methods, limitations and strengths.

4. **Resources:** The Guyanese farmers' field of competences and the quality of their products. Employees' attachment to their territory. Great emotional intelligence.

5. **Effects:** To have a better life and work together. Contribute to the development of the territory and the well-being of the people who live and work there.

Summary

Communication Skills

Presentation Skills

Facilitation Skills

Emotional Intelligence

Influencing Skills

Last, but not least, let's highlight which of the nine generative consulting competences were most vital in order to establish and maintain a generative state of creative flow in all of the relevant actors. We were working in a context where there had been loss of identity and meaning, where social conflicts were very present and where there was a very low level of trust. There were also significant intercultural dynamics to be addressed. Thus, the most important skills in this context were those related to **communication, presentation** and **facilitation. Emotional intelligence** and **influencing skills** were also essential to our success.

Moreover, we were operating in the very specific context of restructuring state services, and we did not know what form the final restructuring would take. The intervention was taking place in a country with Indigenous people, whose ways of operating were very different from ours; a country where the wealth of the territory is the object of greed and yet where there is also great poverty. In such a context, it was not possible to apply previously existing models.

This is precisely where the principles and approach of generative consulting are necessary in order to formulate new possibilities and to achieve effective and practical results very quickly. It also highlights the power of using the various facets of the DIAMOND Model to generate multiple interventions over the course of a year.

Essential to the success of the intervention and the reactivation of the client's ability to perform effectively as a collective was the development of individual awareness and people's reclaiming of their individual power. The ability to move ahead with confidence and achieve concrete results in a context of such uncertainty was the result of applying the principles and processes of generative change to promote personal development and the empowerment of the key actors.

4.7 Key messages for generative consultants

* Get your clients out! Create learning journeys for the orga-nization to help people discover what is already possible or might be for them.

* Let your clients in! Help them create a client-centered vision for the future.

* Focus on creating traction by involving as many stakehold-ers as you can, even the ones at the frontiers of the system.

* Facilitate courageous, heart-based discussions address-ing each level of success factors (environment, behaviors, capabilities, values and beliefs, identity, and vision and purpose): motion is created by emotion.

* Create the conditions for people to confront their differenc-es of perception and create new perspectives from there: the difference is generative!

"The difference between level 5 and level 4 leaders is not personality but personal humility – you need to be in service with an indominable will. What's the truth of your personal ambitions? You need to service a cause." *

* Based on a Jim Collins lecture at WOBI
New York in November 2019

Chapter 5

A Practical Approach. How does it all come together?

Mickey A. Feher

5.1 Overview

This is the case of the daughter company of a large Fortune 500 multinational organization who sought help to improve sales effectiveness and deal management as well as to reduce cultural divisions within the management team. In this chapter, I describe how this intervention turned into a generative change program, starting with the leader of the team who hired us and, eventually, extending to the sales team, in order to address their original request to increase deal conversion rates. I also illustrate the importance of establishing big picture clarity by defining purpose, vision, ambition and roles, in order to achieve the desired improvement at an operational level.

> *Everything that irritates us about others can lead us to an understanding of ourselves.*
>
> - Carl Gustav Jung

5.2 Why is this chapter important?

This chapter presents a real-life case study, which illustrates the application of many key elements of generative consulting: the SFM Success MindsetMap, the SFM Leadership Model and the SFM DIAMOND Model for generative consulting.

I have been in the consulting profession since 1996. One consistent theme that I have encountered during this time across multiple industries and geographies was that many people believe that someone else should change and that this will be the solution to their problem. Therefore, most briefs and jobs assignments that you will get as a consultant will be about "fixing" someone else, setting the team right, changing middle management, motivating key contributors, etc. Seldom will the people who have the power to give you the job be conscious of their systemic contribution to their problem. One of the key abilities of a generative consultant is to help clients realize that they are part of the problem and only if they consider changing too will the perceived symptoms become transformed and their desired outcomes and effects be achieved.

The following chapter will show how this tendency manifested itself with a client. I will present how the original request from this client for a traditional consulting job evolved to take on a very different generative focus. I will examine how the seven steps and the nine competences of the SFM DIAMOND Model played a key role in the successful transformation of the client, his team and his company.

Before we go deeper into our case study, let us explore the larger business context we typically operate in as generative consultants.

5.3. The business context around us

It should be noted that we typically operate in a context that is far from favorable for generative consulting. To illustrate this, here is how Milton Friedman started his article published in *The New York Times Magazine*, on September 13, 1970.

> *"When I hear businessmen speak eloquently about the "social responsibilities of business in a free-enterprise system, ... The businessmen believe that they are defending free enterprise when they declaim that business is not concerned "merely" with profit but also with promoting desirable "social" ends; that business has a "social conscience" and takes seriously its responsibilities for providing employment, eliminating discrimination, avoiding pollution and whatever else may be the catchwords of the contemporary crop of reformers. ... Businessmen who talk this way are unwitting puppets of the intellectual forces that have been undermining the basis of a free society these past decades."*

These thoughts have since been shaping corporate America and the rest of the world. They have also been an influential force in how management education and the consulting profession is approached around the world. Now we all know where this kind of thinking got us. The assumption that companies can exist in a vacuum and that their actions do not affect the rest of the system we live in, is just wrong. The idea that leaders and managers should look after profits only and that someone else will take care of their social responsibilities is naive, to say the least.

The financial crisis of 2008-2009 was a moment of possible awakening but it was quickly subdued and corporations went back to their original practices, as the business sector (and governments) clearly failed to take any strong (legislative) actions to prevent another crisis from arising.

However, in September 2019, 200 chief executives, including the leaders of Apple, Pepsi and Walmart all part of the so-called the Business Roundtable, issued a statement on "the purpose of a corporation," arguing that companies should no longer advance only the interests of shareholders. According to the group, they must also invest in their employees, protect the environment and deal fairly and ethically with their suppliers. They stated:

"While each of our individual companies serves its own corporate purpose, we share a fundamental commitment to all of our stakeholders," the group, a lobbying organization that represents many of America's largest companies, said in a statement . . .We commit to deliver value to all of them, for the future success of our companies, our communities and our country."

Does this mean that the business sector is finally coming to its senses and that business leaders are now interested in what is going to happen to the world, the environment and our communities?

Although we like to talk about the economy and the market as abstract concepts, in reality it is the leaders and people in the companies whose mindset needs to change, one at a time. As the world was reminded by psychologist Viktor Frankl back in 1945 – we cannot live a healthy life without finding meaning. Furthermore, once we find that meaning, we can survive even the worst sufferings, like the Holocaust. Based on my personal experience as a leader and psychologist, I have long believed this to be true for the economy (holon) as well. Even though it took almost 60 years, research has clearly shown that purpose-oriented employees, organizations and entrepreneurs are more likely to perform better and thrive.

I once worked with the top management team of a multinational company and we were discussing what motivated them – why they worked. One of the top executives whose entire management team was also present, admitted doing the job for the money only. The declared goal of the workshop was to work on the Vision and Mission of the organization and the team... Everybody froze as this answer was hardly an inspiration for the others; no authentic work was possible from that point on. This particular experience and many others guided me to realizing the relevance of purpose in a business and I have been teaching people what I deeply believe myself – that living without purpose is like flying a plane blindfolded, which typically ends badly.

Based on a survey published in 2017 in the USA by *Imperative*, employees can be easily classified into two categories. There are employees for whom work is only about money and personal status – i.e., non-purpose oriented. Alternatively, there are employees who see work as a way to empower others, create value and find personal fulfillment. In other words, they are purpose oriented.

This orientation is a key motivational style and attitude, independent from the level of one's position. Purpose-oriented employees perform much better, become more effective leaders, remain with the organization for a long time and have better relations with their colleagues – all of which drive higher engagement.

Such "next-generation entrepreneurs" are the businesspeople of the future. According to the 2016 Cone Communications Millennial Employee Engagement Study, 70 % of the employees around the world look very carefully at the environmental and social impact of an organization before choosing to work there. According to LinkedIn's 2018 Workplace Culture report, nearly nine out of ten, or 86 percent, of millennials (those between the ages of 22 and 37 today) would consider taking a pay cut to work at a company whose mission and values align with their own. By contrast, only 9 percent of baby boomers (those currently between the ages of 54 and 72) would. And by 2025, Generation Y (millennial) employees will constitute 75 % of the world's total workforce.

Our own research with Success Factor Modeling shows that next generation entrepreneurs look for a combination of purpose and clear identity. These entrepreneurs define themselves as explorers, catalysts, networkers and co-creators, reflecting the importance of change and creativity. They are purpose-oriented; this drives their passion and high energy. Interestingly, they have a lot in common with Generation Y in this respect; a values orientation is typical for both of these groups.

A number of well-known businesspeople have shared similar thoughts about this. Richard Branson talks about *"Taking on massive, seemingly impossible challenges"* while wanting to *"life live to the full..."* Elon Musk thinks *"we should aspire to increase the scope and scale of human consciousness in order to better understand what questions to ask and to achieve greater collective enlightenment".*

Interestingly, very few organizations seek consultants to help them define their purpose. Most businesses will have other stated explicit objectives that are related to profit and perhaps some key performance indicators (KPIs) that they perceive as directly connected to profitability. It is one of the jobs of the generative consultant to encourage their clients to explore the deeper issue of purpose.

The following case study describes this process and its challenges.

5.4 The brief we received

I am sitting in a very modern office in the Dumbo office complex, in NYC. The windows overlook the water and I can see the Brooklyn Bridge from the window.

The managing director (we will call him "John") walks in. He explains that he has a division management team of eight people, each leading own teams. Four of the team members also have very high-level key account management responsibilities. Their conversion rates are very low (turning prospects into contracted agreements),and the sales cycles are way too long, he states, visibly irritated.

In order to give me further context, he explains that they are the US daughter company of large global business headquartered in Sweden. The mother company provides a certain framework in terms of brand, values and high-level strategy, but they are not involved deeply in running the US business. The people on the team were coming from two different companies and two different cultures. Three people on the team came from the Swedish company while the majority of the team were American (including the division head).

At the end of the meeting John hands me a set of written goals:

* Increase cohesiveness in his team and get rid of legacy thinking

* Get rid of silo thinking and bring in more collaboration

* Build clarity around good management practice and turn managers into effective leaders who can coach

* Ultimately increase sales (reduce sales cycle and increase conversion rate)

5.5 What we made of the brief

One of the key axioms in the generative approach to conscious leadership is that generative consultants work from the inside-out in terms of how to impact key stakeholders. If you look at the brief, all the goals go according to the usual themes, they are about "fixing" the people on the team, correcting their behavior, etc.

As we truly believe that change has to come from the top and that symptoms come from a systemic interference which includes the leader, our recommendation was that the development process should start with some individual executive coaching with the CEO/head of division.

As we stated in Chapter 1, SFM asserts that our *mindset* produces the *actions* we take, which in turn bring about *outcomes* and achievements.

The Basic Success Factor Modeling Template

Based on some of the initial interviews with John, I felt that he might have multiple objectives that were in conflict with each other. Namely, he stated that his key goal was to scale the business and build robust processes for execution and effective coaching. But I felt that he himself was concerned with something else; which was to increase his personal satisfaction in what he was doing. He was not conscious of this at all at the beginning of the process, so coaching was crucial.

I needed to convince John that the change work should start with him before we addressed the team needs. I managed to do this by appealing to his strategic mind and pride by saying that he needed to drive this forward more than anyone. Hence, he needed to be 100% clear on his own vision.

5.6 John's Success Mindset Map

As introduced in the chapter on Stimulating Growth, the SFM Success MindetMap™ tool is designed to help us understand whether somebody's mindset supports achieving the goals they have set for themselves and how their mindset compares to other successful leaders. The Success MindsetMap™ tool is equally applicable to a business owner or entrepreneur as it is to a leader in a large organization.

To create the map, we applied the distinctions of Success Factor Modeling to analyze well-known entrepreneurs such as Elon Musk of Tesla, Steve Jobs of Apple, Richard Branson of the Virgin Group, Jeff Bezos of Amazon.com, Howard Schultz of Starbucks, Muhammed Yunus of Grameen Bank, Anita Roddick of The Body Shop, and many others.

The MindsetMap helps people to identify their particular aptitudes and tendencies and to know which ones they need to prioritize and strengthen in order to take their project or venture to the next level.

Meta Mindset – Big Picture Clarity

As we pointed out in Chapter 2, Meta Mindset relates to success factors at the levels of purpose and identity and has to do with our fundamental attitude toward our work, our world and our place in that world. To help clarify and enrich each element of Meta Mindset, Robert Dilts and I have selected a well-known entrepreneur who typifies each aspect of Meta Mindset to serve as a type of role model.

Starting a new venture or driving an existing one forward into the future is also very much like the journeys taken by the early explorers. They needed to have a certain mindset and appropriate tools in order to reach their desired destinations.

Let us explore John's Meta Mindset with the following six elements.

1st Element: Know what you really love to do

The Success MindsetMap™ questions	John's Answers
What do you really love to do?	I love building something new, but less so to maintain and sustain a well-oiled machine
What are you excited about?	About new ventures and projects
What is interesting and compelling for you?	To figure out the next step, the next project and get it off the ground
What brings you a deep sense of enthusiasm and energy?	To figure out the next step, the next project and get it off the ground

2nd Element: Know what you want to help create in the longer-term future (Are clear about your destination; and your longer-term vision)

Vision can best be defined as "a mental image of what the future will or could be like." The creative vision of a leader has to do with this ability to imagine and focus on longer-term possibilities that improve people's lives in some way. It involves the ability to see beyond the confines of the "here and now" and imagine future scenarios. It also involves the capacity to set and stay focused on longer-term goals and adopting long-term plans and a holistic view.

John was very focused on what the current situation was in the company and how he was being "played out" by members of the senior management team. He needed to think about his longer-term future in order to realize that he was more interested in building many ventures then managing a single company.

The Success MindsetMap™ Questions	John's Answers
What do you want to create in the world through you that is beyond you?	He essentially described a group of successful green entrepreneurs succeeding to make the world a more sustainable place
What is the world to which you want to belong?	A world that relies on green energy

3rd Element: Are clear about your direction, regardless of whether or not you know the ultimate destination.

Vision is about looking into the future to see you want to create in the world through your venture. This can be more challenging if you are not entrepreneur but work inside an organization.

John had a distant image of the future that was very unclear and did not see a path or a direction leading from his current state to that point in time. His life was completely out of balance and he found it hard to imagine using his best abilities in his current role.

4th Element: Know your purpose – know what you stand for and why you are doing what you are doing.

John found this area particularly challenging as he had not ever thought about his purpose before.

As a result exploring some of the coaching questions, he was able to come to the following realizations:

The Success MindsetMap™ Questions	John's Answers
What is your service to the bigger system and vision?	John saw himself as the eye for spotting the right opportunities to make a difference regarding societal-level environmental issues. His service was to actually build or help build ventures that address these issues
What is your unique contribution to making the vision happen?	The ability to pull together a team and start a business.
What are the special gifts, resources, capabilities and actions that you bring to the larger system in order to help reach the vision?	Strategic vision and planning skills; recruiting the right talent, structuring information in a convincing and inspiring manner.

5th element: Are clear about your ambition – what you want to become and achieve in the next two to five years.

Ambition is a result of the desire and determination to achieve success and recognition for oneself. Ambition is defined as "a strong desire to do or to achieve something, typically requiring determination and hard work" that brings us personal benefit. In spite of his initial rating of "9", John was not very clear on this. Once he realized that he actually wanted to leave the business in two years, it was as if a fog lifted. Suddenly, he was able to think about the necessary steps needed to succeed in his current role and then to look beyond it in order to define a business and role as an investor as his next steps.

The Success MindsetMap™ Questions	John's Answers
What type of life do you want to create for yourself?	A life with more freedom – run his own firm rather than being part of a large corporation.
What do you want to accomplish? What type of status and performance do you want to achieve with respect to yourself and others?	CEO role rather than head of a division
What would you like to be recognized and/or remembered for? What would you like to be able to add to your resume or biography?	Be an investor working with multiple businesses all aiming at the sustainability field

6th Element: Are clear about your role – the position you have with respect to others in your market/environment.

Role is defined as "the function assumed, or part played by a person in a particular situation." Thus, roles are related to both "function"—which is based upon competence—and "the part played"—which is determined by one's position or status. In other words, a role reflects personal skills, abilities, and efforts. John realized that he was a great mentor and starter, and less of a finisher.

The Success MindsetMap™ Questions	John's Answers
What type of person do you need to be and what role do you need to have in order to create the life you want and succeed in your ambition? Mission? Vision?	John realized that he needed to be more proactive and take things into his own hands by paving his way out of the business while also setting up his own team for success.
What is your position with respect to others in your environment/market?	John was seen as an outsider in the company, due to his style and previous higher role.
What are the core competences you need to be the type of person you need to or to achieve and remain in the necessary position or status?	We identified resilience, influencing skills and team building as the most important competences.

Macro Mindset – Habits of success

 As stated in Chapter 2, Macro Mindset relates to the mental disciplines and practices required to bring focus to the big picture of your venture and begin putting it into action. Like lifting barbells, such practices strengthen the mental discipline necessary for sustainable success. These involve such capabilities as managing your energy and focus, seeking honest and frequent feedback, scanning for opportunities, dealing effectively with risks and adversity, and recharging and balancing yourself.

John realized that in his current position he was forced to move to a more operational management role which was far from his passion for starting new things. He also realized that he needed to develop more of the means and the discipline to be able to take care of himself and not become overly stressed or burned out. Further, it became clear to him that he was guessing a lot about what his superiors and peers thought about him rather than having established channels for quality feedback from them.

Micro Mindset – Ongoing Priorities

 Our Micro Mindset produces and guides the specific actions necessary build a sustainable venture. The Micro Mindset of successful entrepreneurs and leaders is a function of identifying their ongoing priorities with respect to nine critical actions. These include

1. Setting aside the time to explore and reconnect with what you love to do, what is important to you and what you are good at doing – i.e., your passion, your sense of purpose and your area of excellence.

2. Creating opportunities for ongoing dialog with customers and prospects.

3. Brainstorming and implementing products and services that anticipate and fulfill customer needs.

4. Attracting and providing direction and support to team members and encouraging team cooperation.

5. Encouraging and providing opportunities for team members to learn and grow.

6. Identifying potential investors and providers of other essential resources and creatively getting their interest and commitment to support your venture.

7. Creating and developing a sustainable infrastructure and a path for growth and scalability of your venture.

8. Seeking and establishing win-win relationships with potential partners and allies who resonate with your values and vision.

9. Identifying and leveraging synergies between what you are doing and the products, services or competences of other ventures.

John felt that he enjoyed and was good at almost all these actions. He had not, however, been making the time to do the following:

* Explore and reconnect with his passion, his sense of purpose and his area of excellence;

* Brainstorm and implement products and services that anticipate and fulfill customer needs;

* Attract and provide direction and support to team members, and encourage team cooperation.

These became his new ongoing priorities.

[Note: See *Appendix III* for the detailed results of John's MindsetMap.]

Meta Goals – Current Focus

The final distinction needed to complete John's Success MindsetMap was to identify his meta goal. Meta goals are our current focus. Even though there were many important goals John was working on, the key was to identify the most important one.

John initially identified *Building a Scalable Business* as his key objective. However, after some individual coaching he opened up and admitted that he had lost much of his personal satisfaction in what he is doing as managing director of the division. Therefore, we agreed that his real meta goal was *Reconnecting to his Passion and Purpose* and *Increasing his Motivation*.

Applying the Mindset Compass to John's Case

Putting all of the pieces of the MindsetMap—Meta Mindset, Macro Mindset, Micro Mindset and Meta Goals—together with respect to the Circle of Success, we can summarize the overall Success Mindset Map™ in a diagram.

The Success Mindset Map™ below, for example, is the ideal mindset for John's meta goal of *Increasing Personal Satisfaction*:

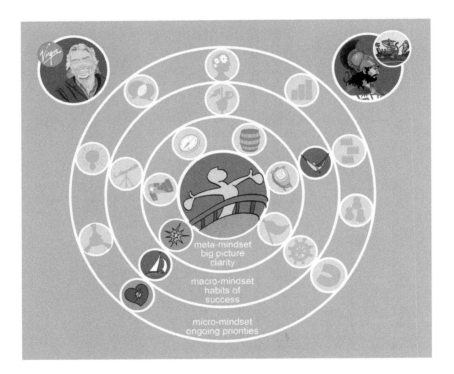

As we can see on the above map, in order to increase personal satisfaction in what you are doing, you need to adopt a mindset like Richard Branson of the Virgin Group. You need to "follow your passions – in a way that serves the world and you."

You also need to have a "lust for adventure" like the mythical travel-er Ulysses and feel the desire to strive, to seek, to find and not to yield."

However, John's actual Mindset Map, in this case, was the following:

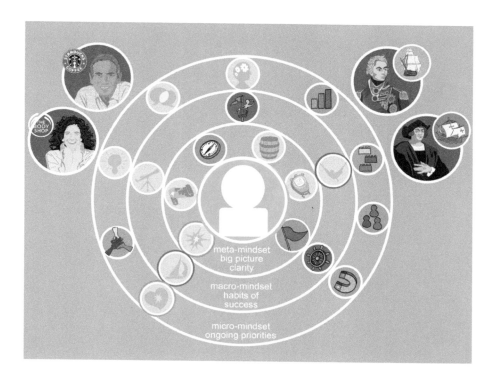

What we discovered was that John's mindset was ideally oriented to achieving financial robustness and stability as he had a great "Finan-sourcerer" and "MarketMaker" mindset. However, the challenge was that he was not able to play his role authentically. People didn't feel the spark in him anymore, especially, since they could compare his current behavior to previous times, before the merger.

The Direction of Generative Change Required in John's Case

John needed to increase his ability to be totally in touch with the *spark* that came from connecting with his passion. The key to this was to figure out what that was,

Although we knew that John would need a greater level or energy and motivation for his current role and venture to help him to go "full sail" for what he wanted, in this particular case it was not possible. The classical management consulting approach would not be able to handle a situation like that. It would be considered an inappropriate conversation and it would never happen, or if it did, it would be politely ignored,

However, in our case this discovery actually helped all parties involved. Given that the contract was basically between three parties (the business itself, the coachee and the coach) the question was, "How we can build a generative solution that will satisfy all three involved?",

By helping John to hone in on his three-year vision, which was clearly oriented outside of the company, he paradoxically regained his strength and motivation to make the changes he needed in order to succeed within his current company context. He knew that he needed to train a successor, and he was also willing to make some tougher decisions he had been hesitating about for a while,

As often happens, we also found out that he needed to develop more of the means and the discipline to be able to take care of himself and prevent becoming overly stressed or burned out. In order to do that, he needed to set aside more time to explore and reconnect with what he loved to do, what was important to him and what he was good at doing – i.e., his passion, his sense of purpose and his area of excellence.

The Cultural elements

As we stated in Chapter 1, in generative consulting we are always looking at how each part of a holon fits into the larger holarchy. One of the primary challenges faced by John and his team were the cultural differences between the US-based daughter company and the Swedish parent organization. To help address this, we applied Geert Hofstede's *Theory of Cultural Dimensions*[1] to examine how these cultural differences might affect the relational dynamics among team members.

---

1   Hofstede, Geert (2001). *Culture's Consequences: comparing values, behaviors, institutions, and organizations across nations* (2nd ed.). Thousand Oaks, CA: SAGE Publications. ISBN 978-0-8039-7323-7. OCLC 45093960.

The Hofstede model of national culture consists of six dimensions. These dimensions represent independent preferences for one state of affairs over another that distinguish country cultures (rather than individuals) from each other. The model includes the following dimensions:

Power Distance Index (PDI)

This dimension expresses how the members of a particular society, and especially those with less power relate to power. In societies with a high power distance index, power is distributed unequally and those with power are less trusted. In low PDI societies, power is distributed more equally and people with power are more accepted.

Individualism versus Collectivism (IDV)

Societies and cultures with high IDV prefer a loosely-knit social framework in which individuals are expected to take care of only themselves and their immediate families. On the other hand, in a more collectivist culture, individuals can expect their relatives or team members of a group to look after each other. A culture's position on this dimension is reflected in whether people identify themselves in terms of "I" or "we."

Masculinity vs Femininity (MAS)

More masculine cultures are characterized by strongly valuing achievement, heroism, assertiveness, and material rewards for success. These cultures are very competitive. Whereas, more feminine cultures place high value on cooperation, modesty, caring for the weak and quality of life. These cultures are less competitive and consensus oriented. In the business context masculinity versus femininity is sometimes also related to as "tough versus tender" cultures.

Uncertainty Avoidance Index (UAI)

This dimension indicates how members of a culture feel about uncertainty and ambiguity. Teams, cultures and societies with a high UAI are more strict and rigid and intolerant. Low UAI cultures are more easy going, less control oriented and more tolerant.

Long-term vs Short-term Orientation (LTO)

Low LTO cultures are more traditional and have many norms with an often suspicious and more negative view towards change. Cultures high on LTO, on the other hand, tend to be pragmatic, progressive and future oriented.

Indulgence vs Restraint (IVR)

Indulgence stands for a society that allows the relatively free gratification of basic and natural human drives related to enjoying life and having fun. Restraint stands for a society that suppresses gratification of needs and regulates it by means of strict social norms.

Below is a summary of how the United States and Sweden score with respect to the factors listed above.

Country Comparison

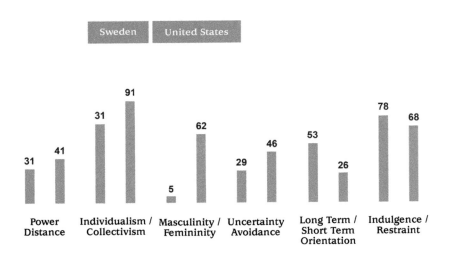

As you can see, the main cultural differences relate to masculinity, with the US being significantly more masculine than Sweden. There are also notable differences in that Swedish people tend to be more long-term oriented and they don't handle uncertainty quite as well as Americans.

In this case, the main challenge was that John was American and the two members of his team who were Swedish found his style too "tough." His assessment of them was that they were not tough enough for the job. There was also the issue of dealing with other teams who were based in Sweden. There were many communication "hiccups" and misunderstandings around the "let's get stuff done" American attitude versus the softer and more indulgent Swedish approach.

There were also issues regarding the long-term Swedish orientation versus the short-term American approach of seeking the "low-hanging fruit."

The main goal of our intervention was for John and his team members to be become more self-aware of these tendencies and to be able to discuss their differences in a more objective manner, as opposed to throwing out personal interpretations and opinions which tended to create many conflicts between team members. We will present more on our approach to this in the remainder of this chapter.

How the generative consulting competences were applied in this project

I thought it would be useful for other generative consultants if I took some of the competences scorecards and their self-reflection questions and answered all the questions in connection with our approach for this project. I used the generative coaching process for John as the main focus of reflection. However, these answers are also relevant with regard to the interactions we had with other key stakeholders during our interventions.

1. Pattern Detection Skills

Questions	Self-Reflections
1. On which levels (environment, behavior, capabilities, values and beliefs, identity and purpose) were there potential patterns?	Based on our initial discussion, John's focus was entirely on behaviors of others ,and the need he expressed was centered around improving the skills of the team members.
2. What kind of links did you make between information given and your personal observations?	I observed that John's body language changed and his level of tension relaxed when he was talking about his past successes working for other companies.

2. Communication skills-

Questions	Self-Reflections
1. How did you adapt your communication style to address all of types and levels of people involved in the interaction?	Initially the key was to be able to relate to John. He needed to feel comfortable that the program could address some of his key issues regarding the number of deals his teams were able to close. This was the main contributor to the profitability of the business and he was measured mainly on that KPI.

However, I spent a significant amount of time to building rapport with him. |
| 2. What did you do in order to perceive and respond quickly to both verbal and non-verbal feedback? | During the conversation I was careful to mirror him and match his energy level. I also paid close attention to my own COACH state and breathing. |
| 3. What kind of verbal reframing did you use to bring new perspectives to the situations being discussed? | I used the "as if frame" a lot, asking questions like, "If you were to do this, what would happen?" |

Strategic Thinking

Questions	Self-Reflections
1. How did you ensure that your client was not only focusing on the next steps (destination) but also keeping consistent attention on the bigger picture (longer-term direction)?	For all 3 three questions the key was to shift John's attention from a short-term "fix-it" orientation to focusing on himself first, and then to the bigger picture view of the vision. I achieved this by helping him realize how his own (lack) of personal vision was the barrier to re-energizing the organization's drive for productivity.
2. How did you ensure that ambitions were aligned with the larger vision?	The vision included ambitions, but also an intended impact on the environment and customers which strengthened the "soul" side of the organization.
3. How did you use both details and knowledge about the bigger picture to build a critical path leading to both the ambition and the vision?	We connected the results and the details of deal management to achieving a larger-context vision which helped to highlight the reason why to make changes to processes.

Systemic Thinking

Questions	Self-Reflections
1. How many different perceptual positions did you acknowledge and include in your interactions?	It was very helpful that I had done many previous sales transformation projects and knew that salespeople are often opposed to the types of changes that a new best practice in deal management brings about. It was thus much easier to get their buy-in by focusing on building a common vision, which was both compelling and realistic from their point of view as well.
2. How frequently did you make reference to and draw attention to the bigger picture and long-term consequences of the subject of your interactions?	
3. Did you maintain a balance of attention between the individual parts and the whole system during your interactions?	

Influencing Skills

Questions	Self-Reflections
1. Were you able to maintain a generative state in yourself and others during the interactions irrespective of how smooth or challenging they were?	It was actually quite challenging to not get caught up with the initial nay-sayings and assume that the organization didn't have openness for larger-scale vision and purpose work.
2. How effectively did you seek and respond to the positive intention behind disagreements or resistance?	Our strategy there was to gain alignment with the top manager involved in sponsoring the program by giving him invaluable help to set his agenda and purpose in the right direction.
3. Were you able to reframe disagreements and resistance into valuable insights for a more inclusive solution?	We used supervision to carry out the process and sometimes faced resistance. The supervision work and applying the four perceptual positions technique proved invaluable throughout the whole process.

How we applied the seven steps of the Generative Consulting DIAMOND Model

1. Defining the Present State: Gathering information and diagnosing the current situation

Here we decided to use a range of qualitative and quantitative tools.

* John's Success MindsetMap™
* PCM personality profiles
* In-depth interviews
* Focus groups

This process included:

a) Diagnostic interviews; focus groups; 360 survey

Most consulting engagements start with similar diagnostic steps. The key difference in our case was that we paid attention to certain factors that would be overlooked by ordinary consulting approaches. These factors included individual mindsets, cultural DNA, non-verbal behaviors and, primarily, the fact that we used the SFM Leadership Model and the Success MindsetMap™ as our guiding structures.

b) Diagnostic report

This report was presented to John and to head of Human Resources (HR). After the presentation we asked for some one-to-one time with John and proposed that individual coaching with him would be the best way to start. We explained that he needed to be a walking example of the purpose and vision we were about to create together. Also, we explained that we always used personal purpose and vision as a starting point. He accepted the reasoning and we agreed on a personal coaching process with six sessions.

As a result of the diagnostic process, we come up with the following SCORE chart for the organization.

SCORE diagnostic for John

Symptoms	Possible Causes		Desired Outcomes	Resources	Effects
	Outer	Inner			
High churn rate	Highly competitive and new industry	Demotivated MD	• Motivated team • Low churn rate	Team was once more united – reference memories	Team achieving together
Missed deadlines	Broken promises regarding the MD's compensation package	Belief that Vision cannot be defined	Higher conversion rates		Greater optimism
Rivalry and politics	Belief that everyone is best off alone	Unclear common purpose for management team	Innovative ideas	Some projects brought people together	People reaching out for help
Leadership not perceived effective in terms of quality feedback	Infrequent feedback	Belief that management is too high up to see real issues in the workplace	Leadership perceived as competent	John's ability to become more congruent	Open communication and feedback upward and downward

In this case, we had to deal with multiple challenges from a leadership point of view.

* First of all, there was no clear vision or ambition established for this team. It was unclear what results and objectives they wanted to reach within a five-year time frame. They had annual individual objectives, but they did not share those with one another.

* Given that they only had individual goals, they had not discussed their interdependencies and their common goals as a team.

* The team had no clear purpose statement. As a result, there was very little cooperation and high levels of competitiveness amongst the team members.

* The MD himself was demotivated and unable to be a positive example of a highly spirited, effective, innovative leader, which is what he expected from others on the team.

2. Intention Setting: Establishing the desired state/direction for change

The key issue for John was that he needed to see his own future more clearly. Taking him through the Success MindSet Map led to the following results:

* John realized that he was not connected to his passion and not clear on his purpose

* Once he was clearer on his purpose, he decided that he needed to build a legacy and train his successor

* We helped him to identify a successor and proceeded to work on a vision document for the organization.

* We worked on a VMAR (Vision, Mission, Ambition, Role) document with him and then repeated this exercise with his team. The team, however, did not see John's VMAR until they completed their own version during a facilitated workshop.

3. Action Planning: Building a critical path

This included taking John through the generative coaching process. As he was able to see his future more clearly, he realized that he needed to find his successor and coach her/him to be able to take over from him in ten to twelve months.

Once this was clear we were able to build a completely new development process for his team which included:

a. Defining the team vision and purpose (through a series of team coaching workshops);

b. Connecting company values to their vision (one-on-one consulting sessions with HR and John);

c. Discussing vision/mission/ambition and setting objectives in line with the vision (team coaching workshop)

d. Discussing roles and key competences (one-on-one sessions between John and his team members, shadowed by our coaches)

e. Developing competences and introducing an ongoing on-the-job coaching system for the organizations managers (with follow-up coaching from HR and a designated internal project manager)

f. Developing a best practice sharing process (eight steps outlining effective strategies and preparation; effective account planning; setting meeting objectives; effective presentation and offering reframing insights to the client; closing and follow-up. This was done through individual interviews, shadowing and a team workshop with selected top-performing negotiators facilitated by our coach)

4. Moving into Action: Executing the plan

The program was a multi-step process:

a) Individual coaching of John

This was perhaps the biggest differentiator, in John's opinion, as to what made this intervention distinct and more generative than other previous consulting support he had experienced. He said that the generative coaching process really produced the spark he needed to propel the organization forward. He cited the courage of the process and how very personal questions were addressed which would normally be considered off-limits.

The trust we built lasted through the entire intervention and John ought out personal advice and follow-ups beyond the originally agreed coaching sessions.

b) A set of workshops for the leadership team

Another significant difference in terms if our approach was that we did not start with the cultural sensitivity session, though this is what John and HR initially believed would need to be the first thing to address. We maintained that they needed to first work on a common higher purpose for the team and explore how it connected to each individual's personal passion and purpose. We designed seven team-coaching sessions that followed the inside-out logic of generative consulting.

1. **Purpose and Passion session** – We identified a both individual and team-level common purpose, and how it connected to what each individual loved doing

2. **Stakeholder Mapping session** – We clarified who the organization's internal and external stakeholders and customers were and what each of them expected.

3. **Vision Setting session** – Based on the identified stakeholder expectations, we addressed the question of what kind of organization they wanted to create in five years and what were some of its key characteristics. Here we used a Purpose/Vision/Mission/Ambition/Role (PVMAR) sheet, with purpose added as a first element.

4. **Objectives and Responsibilities session** – Based on the collective PVMR, we defined what needed to happen in the following 24 months in order to achieve it. We worked with a timeline and created a set of team objectives. By referencing these shared goals, each team member came up with their individual objectives.

5. **Cultural sensitivity session – Collaboration 1** – At that point we introduced Hofstede's map of different cultural dimensions and explored how the team members experienced those differences. The key objective was to demystify and create a better understanding of these dimensions. This made it possible to reduce the personal edge relating to cultural differences, so that people could see these as natural tendencies rather than individual behaviors to be taken personally. We ended the session with a number of agreements as to how members of the two cultures could adjust their verbal and written communications with one another.

6. Personalities and Team Roles session – Collaboration 2

  a) This session utilized the PCM personality profile to create a common language regarding personality traits, as well communication and stress patterns of the members of the team. We reviewed a team profile and managed to untangle many of the issues which were seen as cultural differences. In time. people realized that most of the patterns they were experiencing and found annoying were in fact differences in personality. They were also able to understand that these differences were a source of variety and could even increase effectiveness if they were channeled properly.

  b) The session ended with a set of agreements that ranged from changing the agenda of their weekly management meetings to agreeing on written and verbal communication rules.

7. Cultural Change Planning session

  a) The objective of this workshop was to identify how purpose and vision were to be communicated to the rest of the team and how they would sustain the process.

  b) The key output was to create a quarterly plan with key milestones for each person and change how management meetings were held to focus on a weekly review of progress with respect to key milestone. We also created an internal team consisting of a sales manager and an HR manager to act as internal change project managers, with the support of one of our coaches.

We decided to put in place three team-coaching follow-ups on a quarterly basis with the leadership team, during which we facilitated a process to review progress towards the vision and the corresponding plan. These meetings were to focus on a quarterly big picture perspective, addressing positive or negative patterns, rather than a more operational weekly focus.

As a new thread of work, we agreed on defining a best practice for the deal management process (discussing and using the best practices of the most successful deal makers on the team). This process included the following steps:

* Creating a documentation form

* Creating a coaching observation form

* Training managers for effective coaching

* Shadowing managers as they coached and giving them feedback on the quality of their coaching afterwards

* Measuring organizational KPIs (We were aiming to improve the leadership team's approval scores by 10 %.)

* Measuring Sales KPIs (We were aiming to decrease average time to close a deal by 30 days.)

5. Obstacle Transforming: Dealing with challenges and pitfalls

We encountered many obstacles throughout this process. They were mainly related to other leaders in the company being initially skeptical about the value of the program and criticizing the fact that we did not simply focus on increasing sales results and fixing the deal management process. Thanks to having established a strong alliance with John, and taking every opportunity to present the rationale for the entire program, we were able to overcome most of these objections. We used many generative change methods, such as COACH state, and the generative coaching process for ourselves as well.

On another level, one of our goals was to increase the capacity for resilience of the people with whom we worked. So we taught the team to deal with obstacles using several generative practices:

* Mindfulness practices at the beginning of meetings (e.g., COACH state and others)

* The four perceptual positions process (to be utilized before making major decisions and entering into high-stake negotiations, as a way to prepare)

* The TetraLemma process (for John to learn how to deal with ambiguity and increase resilience while remaining congruent)

6. Noting Progress: Assessing and measuring change

We measured change using several methods:

* Employee engagement surveys (every 12 months)

* Annual churn numbers

* Monthly KPI numbers for sales

* Feedback surveys every quarter (to determine how staff perceived the quality of the managerial coaching they received)

7. Deepening Practices: Follow up for sustaining and deepening the changes

We set up an 18-month-long process. Team members had the option of opting out after each phase.

Most of our work focused on establishing new practices supporting collaboration, communication and dealing with obstacles. Several aspects of this process have been detailed in the previous description of the seven steps of the Generative Consulting DIAMOND Model.

5.7 Conclusion and key messages

The generative consulting approach is based on a methodology, but it is also very much about what the generative consultant personally brings into his or her work. If we consider the various levels of success factors identified in Chapter 1, it is very important that a generative consultant is clear on his or her own higher purpose and identity, and has a set of values that supports generativity. A key prerequisite is that we don't only work with the short-term operational goals we are given, but are also willing to work with the DNA of the organization, which relates to its purpose, vision, mission and ambition (PVMA). The key individuals and stakeholders have their own PVMA and the organization's symptoms and objectives will not make sense without mapping out the mindset of those who are involved in making decisions.

In this chapter I have intended to show that a first brief is seldom going to describe what the organization really needs. It tends to focus more on symptoms rather than on the underlying causes. The key is to be able to take the initial requirements and show how they relate to deeper root causes.

A primary difference between generative consulting and the traditional consulting approach is the conscious management of the consultant's own internal state as well as attending to the inner state of the others involved in the interventions. You can design the right process and put together the right set of questions and yet get poor-quality results if you or the others involved in the process are in a poor quality internal state. One of the purposes of the nine generative consulting competences is to be sure that we and our clients are interacting from a generative state.

This highlights a key principle of generative consulting – that we are always working from the inside out and paying attention to the "inner game" as we address the "outer game." To achieve this, generative consultants have an additional set of tools available that are substantially different from those of traditional consultants.

When John saw his results, these were his words:

"I never thought of my mindset as something that I could analyze and reset according to my goals. I always believed that I can make decisions but cannot change my beliefs.

These results really helped me look in the mirror and get clarity on what I want to change about my current mindset."

- John
Managing Director

"Be the change you want to see in the world."
Mahatma Ghandi

Chapter 6

Being the generative change

Robert B. Dilts, Elisabeth Falcone,
Mickey A. Feher, Colette Normandeau,
Jean-François Thiriet, Kathrin M. Wyss

Robert: *The purpose of this chapter is to get a personal perspective from each of us as authors as to what it meant to participate, not only in writing the book but in living the experiences that led up to the book – about being in addition to doing. The basic topic is **how to be a generative consultant**.*

Jean François: *Our core message is **adaptation to an ever-moving environment**. This is where generativity and our generative work is so important, because solutions that have worked before do not work anymore or cannot work long-term anymore. What used to be a destination can only be seen as a direction these days. We are holding a space for our clients to move through this VUCA world[1] – from vision to action with their teams.*

Kathrin: *I like the notion of the "we" (us) that Jean François brings in. I have experienced that, in the past, big consulting firms just bring their own preexisting solution to the client. This is in contrast to the way we work in generative consulting, which is that we are **with the client, looking together** at the situation. This also means that we as consultants cannot rely solely on our past experiences with other clients. Although, those experiences can give us hints about what to do or take care of with regard to a current client. One of the key things for being generative is to be adaptable and to always stay open to what is there in the moment without judgment, and saying, "I am curious, as I don't know yet what exactly to do with it." So some key questions for a generative consultant are: "How can you stay curious (and open minded) despite all the things that a client may be presenting to you in the form of their perceptions, ideas and assessments? How can you, on one hand, hold space for all of that information for yourself as a consultant and, on the other hand, be the source for holding the space for your client to allow them to open their perspective and be curious rather than judgmental or in despair?"*

Robert: *I would add to that **the importance of multiple intelligences**. I think one of the big challenges, and potential opportunities for businesses, because businesses are primarily built on the rational, linear left brain approach, which makes perfect sense. But it can be very limiting. Especially*

---

1   See Intro Chapter 4 for Definition of VUCA

in this VUCA world, cognitive, rational intelligence is not enough. One of the big challenges for businesses is that of being adaptive and generative, and this requires multiple intelligences. One of our roles as generative consultants is to introduce these other intelligences to our clients and have them realize the absolutely essential importance of them. Somatic intelligence, metaphorical intelligence, relational intelligence, emotional intelligence, etc., are not a "nice to have" there are absolutely necessary. One of my main guidelines has been Einstein's idea that **you cannot solve a problem with the same type of thinking that creates it**. This is one of the reasons that we need to develop and use other intelligences.

Elisabeth: *I would like to add that both* **humans and organizations grow from confronting shadows and difficulties.** *This is important for generativity. As a result of dealing with these challenges, we have more resources, more choices, more possibilities, even if it's not comfortable. With this approach of generativity, we grow in consciousness even if the situation is difficult.*

Mickey: *For me, as I was reading the chapters of our book, and especially as I was writing my own chapter, I made it my internal rule that I should be able to explain why whatever I am describing was different or special.* **Why** *is generative consulting different from classical management consulting? In some ways it has been not so easy to answer the question. You could say that we have the seven-step SFM DIAMOND model. but others will have a five-step model. McKinsey will have a model for this, and BCG a model for that. Consulting companies all come out with their sets of criteria for success, with their set of competencies and their set of processes. How is it possible to differentiate between these models? To me, a key difference is that we are also working with the human software, the mindset, the operating system inside the head. Yet is that differentiating enough? No. There are many other companies that are coming in with the same claim. So, why and how is the generative approach different? Ultimately, it is that we believe that* **the mind is relational**. *What does it mean*

to say "My mind is relational?" It means that my mind is not the same mind if I'm with you versus by myself or with another person. My mind, when I'm with you, is evolving into something that's potentially more than when I am on my own. This is where I think the generativity starts. Now, it's not just about my relationship to my mind and myself and to my body-mind system, but also to yours and to ours as a team. If I'm conscious of that, if I'm able to be aware of the relational field as I'm interacting, then something new, something different is possible. Although I'm applying a process or a tool set, I'm doing it in a relational manner. That's very generative to me.

Colette: *It's interesting to hear all your perspectives. I see the importance of being very agile, flexible and using multiple intelligences, within ourselves and also within a team, within the "we/us," even as we interact with each other here in this discussion. These same characteristics are essential with our clients and for our clients, as we all navigate through life's circumstances and challenges. Every moment is an opportunity to be generative, to stay open to something is new, different and emerging. Kathrin mentioned earlier, holding the space of* **"I don't know"** *and being* **"curious to find out."** *I'm curious where we're going with these questions and discovering what will come out that is also new and different. What thoughts and ideas would not have been there half an hour ago yet can come out now and emerge from this connection among us and these multiple intelligences that are contributing to this field between us. For me, being a generative consultant means really staying open and trusting;* **trusting that in the moment something new will come through.** *Trusting that we have the perfect combination of intelligences here, present within us and in our group to have something emerge.*

Kathrin: *It's having them at your fingertips when you need them and that means* **practice,** *practice, and again practice in times when you don't need them. It's like an airline pilot that is training for emergencies, hoping they never happen. Yet when they do, they know how to perform. For me that's the reason why we have emphasized the nine competences for generative consulting. And, just reinforcing what Mickey said about our mind being relational, one of those areas of*

*competence includes **relational skills** which are needed on multiple levels. Seeing different patterns on a macro level and on the micro level, is also really important. How can we, irrespective of if we are hired externally or if we are working "in-house," maintain the ability to stay detached, allowing us to observe all that is there? It is important to be able to offer feedback such as: "I observed this..." and "I sensed that...," applying the multiple intelligences Robert mentioned to uncover patterns, blind spots, co-dependencies and so on, which our clients possibly don't see. One of the key areas of intelligence I personally apply is that of **aesthetic intelligence** which looks at balance and harmony in systems.*

Robert: *When I look at the three different areas of the Success Factor Modeling – conscious leadership, collective intelligence and next generation entrepreneurship – they are all about living our dreams and making a better world through business. They also share the experience of **connecting to and trusting in something that's bigger than ourselves.** What strikes me about what you were just saying Kathrin, is that it's not a New Age "isn't that a nice idea" attitude. These are core competencies that require a lot of practice and a lot of skill to be able to do, especially in a way that is going to actually help a company to fulfill concrete objectives. This dynamic between a greater consciousness and the concrete world, between dreamer and realist, are extremely key to generative consulting.*

Jean François: *For me, what I really like about our generative work is that it is not only about what we do as a generative consultant, it is also about the mindset that we hold to create that space of emergence. In our mindset, we have premises about this work that are very, very grounded and integrated. I'm alluding to the competence of **systemic thinking and the notion of holons**, which are really key. This is something I really wasn't aware at the beginning of my consulting work that I now consider essential. To me, the health of a system is really based on how much of the holon it can include in its transformation. A sick system is a system that holds part of the holon separate from the rest of the system. The holon is fragmented. What we do as generative consultants is foster*

the ability to develop a systematic perspective. Holding the mindset that we are dealing with holons that are part of bigger holons and helping clients to be more and more aware of these holons makes a real shift in perspective. Elisabeth was talking about the importance of acknowledging the "shadow" in the holon. As generative consultants, we know how to hold that space for the shadow so that light can be brought into it in some way.

Elisabeth: *I like that and I would add that, for us, **the ability to lead, to let go and let come what has to come** in this holon is something fundamental. If we have this ability, we are able to observe that life is much more mysterious. Like you said Robert, it's like a journey that involves practice, the field and our competencies. It's really something much deeper than we realize at first.*

Colette: *I noticed in my experience that generativity comes out when there's a sense of inner security. If I feel secure with my client, and if I've created that space where he/she can also feel secure, then there is place for emergence. It is heavily based on **relational skills**. How do we create that space where magic can come through and that generativity and new ideas can come through? I had a good example recently with a person who was creating challenges for a group I was working with. I had a few people say: "**What are you going to do with this person? She's going to be a disturbance.**" Instead of ignoring or shutting out the person, we took time to connect, to create a relationship, to talk, to be heard and to bond. We found out that she was stuck in her fear which, in turn, awoke fear in other people in the group. By taking time to really connect and talk it out without judgment, we got back to a stronger trust base and felt sense of security. Everything went smoothly for the rest of the time the group was together. It was actually very inspiring and full of generativity, and created space for everybody to express themselves and be creative. I think developing security and trust, and creating confidence by applying our relational skills with our clients is one of the cornerstones of generativity when working with organizations.*

Jean François: *What I really like about what you're saying Colette is that, as generative consultants, we know that the shadow is present in the system and we have* **the ability to work both with shadow and uncertainty** *to help our clients and their teams move through the "not knowing space" with confidence.*

Mickey: *This reminds me of a quote from the movie* Saving Private Ryan: **"This time the mission is the man."** *I remember when I first worked as a management consultant at the beginning of my career, one of the things I was told repeatedly was, "Be careful, don't get too close to your clients, because if you develop a personal relationship, it can interfere with the business, and you're going to screw it up and you're going to be sorry." With generative consulting, we apply the polar opposite of this statement. Every time I have felt that we've been able to make a difference it is because of the relationship and a certain proximity to the client. The experience of resonating together, sharing ourselves, showing up as a full human being and going beyond our role. Think about all these terms that we use, such as* **"systemic intelligence".** *Many people talk about systemic intelligence, but do we know what it is really? To us it's the holon-to-holon connection, and the holon is way beyond the role. It's not just me being a consultant, being here to help a client to come up with a five-year plan. It's you and I, and who are you and who am I, and what are we bringing into this? That is really the key part in so many ways for me.*

Robert: *The word that keeps coming up to me that's key to the whole idea of generative change and generative consulting is* **"connection".** *We can say that essentially disconnection is what creates problems and symptoms, and connection is what creates generativity and solutions. I think a lot of what the generative change work is about is finding connection. This starts with what you were just saying Mickey about the human-to-human connection. It's from there that true ecology emerges and that true collective intelligence and wisdom emerge. As I look back over the chapters of this book that we've been working on, and especially when I look at the case examples, there is a lot of humanity in the work, and a lot of the capacity to find the connections that nobody else is seeing. I think you were just talking about that Mickey. I think*

a lot of our work is to help illuminate the parts of what's happening that are not being either seen or attended to.

Elisabeth: *Yes. At the same time, generative change also involves the ability to* **let go and allow something to come through**. *Even though we have all these competences, practice, are professional and know what we have to do, at one moment we have to let go and see what emerges.*

Colette: *I like that notion of Elisabeth very much. It's the* **"difference that makes the difference".** *It is the difference between knowledge and wisdom. As generative consultants, we can learn, accumulate a lot of knowledge, practice and acquire experience. Wisdom, though, is knowing when to let go, trust and have compassion for the situation, the client and ourselves. Our rational mind knows all the models, steps and key success factors. Our heart can stay compassionate with the actual situation and struggles. It is important to to keep that balance. COACH and CRASH states sound very easy to distinguish on paper. They are not so easy to manage in a dynamic consulting situation.*

Kathrin: *I often challenge myself, in the times when I sense that I am on the verge of going into a CRASH state, to check what is going on for me in relation to each letter of that acronym. That allows me to figure out if it is some type of* **analysis paralysis,** *or the thought "No one likes me," etc. Once I detect what is bringing on the CRASH, I ask myself, "How can I get out of this and back into a COACH state within the next few seconds? And, where can I also detect that pattern within my client?" This makes me think of the notions of assumptions and presuppositions and wonder what kind of presuppositions might be needed to work as a generative consultant.*

Mickey: *The first presupposition that comes to mind that's really key for me as a generative consultant is that* **"fixed filters mean a fixed reality".** *Let's say I am working with a client and see that they are stuck in a particular fixed pattern of mindset. For example, maybe it is a top manager who wants to communicate during a time of crisis, but thinks he must have already gathered all of the data and made a decision before sharing anything. My intention would be to*

show the person how he is stuck in the perceptual position of being "top leadership" and is drawing his conclusions from this one, narrow perspective. These are the times when multiple viewpoints and multiple intelligences become really important. If you are stuck in your own perspective and in your head, trying to do even more of that won't help. I think that, as a generative consultant, having the ability to detect these obstacles created by a fixed mindset is key. We need to be able to take the client with us and move to another source of intelligence; from head to heart or gut, for instance. Help them find new doorways to new interpretations that will lead to new actions.

*Colette: Another presupposition is **"all the resources are in the system".** That's crucial for me. The resources are all there. Kathrin, you were mentioning moving from CRASH to COACH. A few minutes before joining this converstion, I was vacillating between CRASH and COACH. Ultimately, COACH came through. Actually, it was the collective COACH field of this group that got me through the CRASH. Connecting with all of you helped me get back to a COACH state. In an organization it is the same thing. The resources in the system can support and help create that COACH field/state. Earlier, I was reminded of something that Robert shared about 15 years ago. He said, **"To be generative or to be creative we need to unlearn... unlearn what we have been taught are the answers."** How can we unlearn and come back to what is most essential and what wants to come out? I think that in the generative work that we do, it is important to unlearn those fixed patterns and stay open, trust and connect.*

Mickey: Recently, I was facilitating a generative change workshop and we made breakout groups in which the participants were working in a triads. One of the people who was in the role of the coach very skillfully inserted all the right questions that one is supposed to ask under the circumstances. Her objective was to help the coachee to fine tune her vision for her venture. As I observed the conversation, though, I sensed and saw that the coachee was getting increasingly annoyed and tense, and as a result got into a CRASH state. The coachee said she felt self-conscious and like being on an

operating table with observers. What was missing? The coach was asking all the right questions… "What do you want to achieve?" and "What would it do for you to achieve it?" and so on. The relational field was missing and both the coach and coachee were in a poor quality state. This relates to the distinction mentioned at the beginning of this conversation about "being versus doing." I think a key presupposition of generative change is that **it comes more from how you are being than what you are doing.** *My state of consciousness, purpose, identity and beliefs determine the way I am being with you. All these things are happening within me as we speak and I'm aware of them. So, emotional and relational intelligence come more from being than doing.*

Robert: *What comes to me from what you're just saying, as another presupposition of this work, is the idea of complementarity –* **generativity always comes out of a conversation between seeming opposites.** *Elisabeth, you made that beautiful statement about the importance of letting the shadow come into the conversation. Similarly, doing and being can also complement one another and produce something generative. This dynamic shows up in our set of competences. We have relational skills, pattern detection skills, strategic thinking skills, systemic thinking skills, facilitation skills, communication skills, presentation skills and influencing skills. As I apply this set of skills, I'm listening, I'm influencing, I'm thinking in a linear way, I'm thinking in an open way, I'm thinking in a relational way, I'm thinking in a comparing, "finding the difference that makes a difference" way. So, I think this diversity of filters is another big part of what we bring to our clients. A generative consultant is aware of the presence of all of those different ways of perceiving things and the importance of them in not only balancing and offsetting each other but in order to create something new. Through holding paradox, a deeper, more creative innovation can emerge.*

Elisabeth: *For me, there is also the presupposition that* **a generative consultant comes more from his or her own experience than from ideas and theories.** *Each of us has ourselves lived all the steps, all the processes that we are presenting to our clients. We have all lived the path of generative*

change in ourselves and our own businesses and we know from our own experience what we are speaking about. And for me personally, my own path of generative change was an unexpected journey. It was amazing; surprising and amazing.

Jean François: *I relate to what Elizabeth is saying. We were talking about connection to our clients and to the system but effective generative consulting is also a function of how we are connected to ourselves. Another one of our presuppositions is that **the success of our intervention depends on the state we are in and the state of the system that we are working with**. We place a real emphasis on this understanding that "I am a reflection of the holon. I am a reflection of the system. I am an organization myself in some way." This is why my own inner state, my beliefs and the state of my filters are so important to generative consulting.*

Kathrin: *I absolutely agree. This is the concrete meaning of "holon and hologram." The whole is in every part, and we become part of our client's system. As such, our own use of all the multiple intelligences and the degree of harmony and alignment within ourselves is key to our consulting success. This brings up one other point related to "lines of development." **Not every part of a system develops in the same way and in the same time frame.** In situations, such as Elizabeth referred to, when we see shadows in the system, the differences in lines of development between different people and different parts of the holon result in frictions. How can we, as a consultant, working alone or in a team, acknowledge and make space for that; especially in times when not everything is moving along smoothly? How do we set priorities? When do we acknowledge the shadow without addressing it, knowing and trusting that the system indeed has the ability to transform itself? How can we, as generative consultants, open up the system in a way that actually lets all that happen without intervening too much? That is one of the key questions I reflect on most often. Especially in situations when the client asks: "So what are you going to do about it?" My usual answer is "I don't know yet, and I'm curious to find out." For me there is much truth in the saying: "Remaining curious and aware is often 80 % of finding the solution."*

Robert: *That makes sense. I think a lot of what we do and what we are as generative consultants is to act as* **"awakeners."** *By this I mean that we help people to achieve a wider scope of awareness. If the resources are indeed already in the system, why aren't they being used? Usually it is because there is a lack of awareness. Attention is too narrowly focused. We "awaken" them to become aware of the bigger holon and that they are part of that holon. A good example is the case in Mickey's chapter where the managing director realized that he was a type of hologram for his team and his division. He became aware that he was not just some separate individual in his office acting alone, but that actually what was going on in his own mindset impacted the whole system – his mindset was a "difference that made a difference." And once we are awakened, a lot of other things become possible. What we do as generative consultants is intentionally foster this kind of awakening to all parts of the organizational system, or holon.*

Mickey: *The metaphor of a tuning fork comes to mind.* **Ping.** *It creates a pure tone that sets the vibration that all of the participants in the performance (the chorus and musicians) can atune into. And if we start with the right* **resonance** *together we can create a beautiful melody as a team. So maybe that's what we do as generative consultants. We carry the tuning fork that makes it possible for different voices and instruments to interact harmoniously. And if things start to get out of sync then,* **ping.** *We use the tuning fork to help people get back into resonance.*

Colette: *Another thing I have noticed when generativity comes through is that* **we're having fun!** *When we let go and we enjoy working together, there's always something like this tuning fork metaphor or other type of FUN intelligence that comes through.*

Kathrin: *I agree. And I think this is especially important for steps three and four of our DIAMOND model – Action planning and Moving into action.* **Playfulness is essential to a generative mindset.** *One of the things that I always make my clients aware of is that change is never a smooth ride and that they cannot expect it to move in a straight line. It will be more of an organic growth since change, like life, is sometimes very cumbersome.*

*Therefore it is important to build in those playful moments of curiosity and naivety. Like being the little girl or boy that goes to kindergarten, not really knowing yet how to tie your own shoes laces. You see how others are doing it, check what you can do, and maybe you come back with sneakers that don't have traditional shoe laces but Velcro ones. When we, as generative consultants, allow ourselves to demonstrate and build upon all these multiple intelligences in a congruent matter, that's where the fun comes from. So, **dare to be yourself**. Bring in all of yourself and don't try to be someone else.*

Mickey: *Before I became a consultant, I was working as a manager in a big organization. And we hated consultants. We thought "They just come in and we pay them a lot of money. They're going to tell us what to do, and yet they have no real idea what's going on. They have no idea of the context. They don't know the people. They don't understand our business and yet they still tell us what to do." This reflects the notion in traditional consulting that there is this single truth that somebody holds and they can bring it to you. And they're going to tell you, "This is what you're going to have to implement. And if you implement it, you are going to be successful." And everybody knows that is actually a lie, because there is no single truth. As generative consultants, we **hold multiple truths versus a singular truth**. We don't come in and say, "Here's a silver bullet that will fix everything." We say, "There are multiple possibilities. Let us hold the truth of your people, your personal truth, the truth of your Board, the truth of the market reality. Let's work with all of this, stir it in the pot and see what emerges." So, this emergent quality requires humbleness, and it requires dealing with uncertainty. It requires systemic intelligence. And that's very uncomfortable for traditional, left-brain type thinking. This is where generative consulting really ventures into a new territory. Even just to talk about it gives me goosebumps.*

Robert: *To start to bring closure to the conversation, maybe each of us can share some thoughts on the key "differences that make a difference" with generative consulting. We've touched upon a lot of them already, but maybe we can each make a summary statement about that topic.*

Elisabeth: *To me, it's **to be authentic and to live our mission**. It's a question of work, passion and courage. We can't offer or do something with our clients if we haven't first lived it ourselves. For me, it's not about working. It's about passion. We have to be courageous and authentic, and sometimes it's hard. We have to be honest about that as well!*

Colette: *I think it's **leading others as we lead ourselves**. For me a key word is "congruency." How can we stay congruent with what our head, our heart, our mind and our bodies want, and how we can influence through being generative ourselves?*

Kathrin: *Building on this and merging it with the perspective of the "whole and holon," to me it is really important **to create the experience of "we."** If I, as external consultant, can say **"we"** when I talk about a client's generative change process, I bring in my whole self. By asking, "What can we do?" I know that I am within the system and that I can sense the different parts of that system to the degree necessary. If I would always talk about my clients and their teams and stakeholders as **"them"** I would be dissociated from them. For me, this level of disconnection does not allow me to embrace those multiple intelligences enough. Therefore a key for me is, "Can I say **we** when speaking with my clients?"*

Colette: *I'd like to add: "WE" sounds like "OUI" in French which means "YES." And I think that **saying "YES" to what wants to come through** is also very important for generativity to emerge. Saying "YES" to our generative field ~ "OUI to WE."*

Jean François: *To me, as generative consultants, we base our work on processes and not on content. **We are masters of processes, not masters of content**. And that's where humbleness comes in. We don't know all of the answers; we just facilitate the processes. We create the space for generativity to emerge.*

Robert: *When I think about the generative consulting process, I also think about the importance of the different levels of success factors, which we haven't quite touched upon in an explicit way so far ~ environment, behavior, capabilities,*

*values and beliefs, identity and purpose. Working with all of these levels is an explicit part of what we do as generative consultants. Other consultants certainly may end up touching upon these different levels and doing something generative. But I think what's different about what we do is that **we set it up so that all of these levels are explicitly included as a part of the consulting process.** We look at multiple levels and we explicitly look at all the diverse parts of what we're calling the "holon." **We are also explicitly looking for complementarities.** We're bringing in the shadow, as well as the resources for reaching desired outcomes. **We are explicitly bringing awareness and self-awareness to everything that's happening** – not only through what we say, but through how we are. I think part of what makes generative consulting unique are these are things that could potentially happen in any consulting interaction, but are not explicitly built in. It is aways possible for some kind of magical connection between people to occur, but it's what we set out to do intentionally, consciously and explicitly in the generative consulting work.*

Mickey: *As I'm listening to all of you, I agree with each one of you and was wondering if there is anything else that is vital as key component. And what comes to me is that, at any key moment when something is about to happen that's going to be different from what was happening before, you have to **slow down.** So I feel like I constantly remind my clients, as a generative consultant, to "Wait" – to take a little pause to wait and let something brew; to let something emerge that is going to be worthwhile. Because, even though it seems like a time investment at the very moment, it will lead to something that would otherwise never come out, had you not been able to pause. So stop, reflect and listen to what is being said. Then, let's hear other ideas and let's listen to them as well, and stay open to what happens after that.*

Kathrin: *This also reminds me on the importance of **being fully present and having access to all our own resources in every moment.** This is sometimes very difficult because we are applying multiple intelligences ourselves and are multitasking on different levels. Despite all that, we work to*

really be fully present with our clients and their challenges and take the time for something new to emerge.

Elisabeth: *There is also something important in **the way we treat ourselves in our lives**. And that involves our personal disciplines. This might be expressed through a meditation practice, or in what we eat, or how we sleep, for example. I deeply belief that we cannot take ourselves and our clients to another level of being and doing, if we do not apply these disciplines.*

Robert: *Right. How can we know what to do to help our clients with all of these different intelligences if we don't have them and use them ourselves? This connects back to the notion of our being **part of the hologram**. If I don't do it myself, how can I congruently and authentically propose something to another person, or a team or system?*

Elisabeth: *To be the Best of Myself, I have to practice. If I want to reach another level, I have to do something special to increase my abilities.*

Colette: *Something that just came up, that is also part of our uniqueness as generative consultants, is that **we're supporting clients to be aware of and to bring balance to both their soul and their ego**. The ego strives for success; has dreams, goals and objectives. But if the soul is not taken into account, there will be some degree of imbalance and disharmony. The soul seeks to serve a larger mission and vision. Yet if the concrete goals of the organization aren't clearly defined or affirmed, it creates another type of imbalance. I think that, as generative consultants, we contribute to awakening the awareness of the importance of bringing more balance in these two aspects within ourselves and within our clients' organizations.*

Robert: *Thank you Elisabeth and Colette for those last two reflections, because I do think that is part of what makes a generative consultant different from other consultants. I don't think that the big consulting firms suggest that their consultants have some daily practices where they are "practicing what they are teaching." And I'm not sure that they even consider the dynamics of "ego" versus "soul."*

*I think these are also big parts of what makes generative consulting unique. I was thinking of the big organizations that I've consulted for, like Apple, Microsoft, IBM, Fiat, Weight Watchers, etc. Why did they choose me as opposed to one of the big well-known consulting firms? I think it has been because of that generative edge created by these differences that we have been talking about – **multiple intelligences, looking at things on different levels, and this idea of the holon and the whole being in every part.** I think these are really the things that are transformative and, in some ways, revolutionary about generative consulting.*

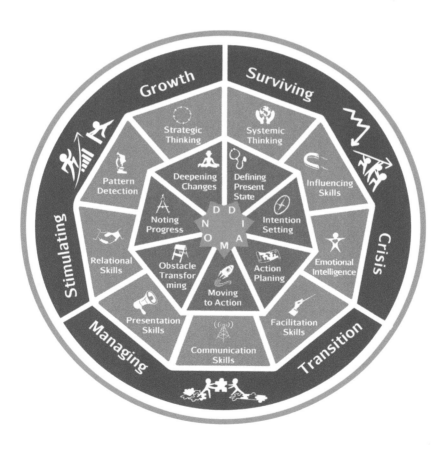

Play with genera

Have Supp
fun!

Master the process not the

Bring your   Find the resour
"be" into
your "do"   Practice being full

Be the SLOW D
generative
change

CREATE
EXPERIE
OF "WE"

Keep in mind the whole
and the holon

m
intel

Become an awaken

ve complementarities

rt the balance
f ego and soul

ontent   Practice to be the best
es within the system   version of
                                      your self

present and resourceful

OWN   Look for complementarities

Look at events through diferent levels

Be authentic and live your
passion and mission

HE
CE   FIND THE DIFFERENCE THAT
        MAKES THE DIFFERENCE

se   Say YES to what wants
tiple   to come through
gences

ACKNOWLEDGE
THE SHADOW

Afterword

Robert B. Dilts

Twenty years ago, my late brother John and I began the adventure of exploring the "differences that made the difference" – the key success factors – that distinguished the most successful individuals, entrepreneurs, leaders, teams and ventures from all of the others. Our goal was to discover the "secret sauce" of success, so to speak, and share our discoveries with the rest of the world.

Having grown up and launched our own careers in the Silicon Valley area of Northern California, John and I were both fascinated by the fact that seemingly average people could create wildly successful ventures so quickly. What used to take years was happening in months or even weeks. It was also obvious that not everyone succeeded. In fact, there were more failures than successes. What made the difference?

We started by looking at some of the obvious Silicon Valley success stories and by interviewing some of our clients and acquaintances who had built successful ventures. A number of key patterns emerged that we organized into what we called the "Circle of Success." In addition to their goals, competencies and actions, we discovered that the most crucial success factors these individuals shared had to do with qualities of mindset, such as having a deep passion, a clear vision, a strong sense of mission and a burning ambition for what they were doing.

A major part of our exploration also included developing principles, practices and processes based on what we had learned that awakened, instilled and strengthened these key success factors in individuals and teams that wanted to increase their capacity for success and take their ventures to a new level.

As we shared what we were learning with our colleagues and friends, they became fascinated and wanted to know what we were doing and what we called it. We decided to name this exploration *"Success Factor Modeling"* – or *SFM* for short.

We began to experiment with our ideas and put them into action. John and I would both interview and coach entrepreneurs who were interested in getting funding for their ideas. It began to become more and more obvious to us what successful entrepreneurs did, how they thought and what motivated them. We came to view an explosion of visionary entrepreneurs and business leaders as the being most certain way to bring positive change into the world; in a way that governments, religions, big businesses and other large institutions would never be able to accomplish.

We began to think of our work with Success Factor Modeling as something more than just knowledge about doing effective business, but rather as a *movement* that would help to enrich people's lives and make a better world. In fact, as we expanded our studies, it became obvious that "success" had not only to do with launching a profitable business, but also included having a thriving family life, loving relationships, flourishing health and a good heart. A core premise of Success Factor Modeling, in fact, is that, in order to grow our professional career or venture, we must also grow and evolve personally. To take our professions, our ventures or our lives to the next level, we have to significantly shift our mindset. That mindset that brought us where we are today will not take us to the next stage. In order to contribute more, we have to grow more.

It has been two decades now that I have been applying and enriching the principles, skills and models identified by the Success Factor Modeling approach. In addition to my own ventures, I (and many others) have used the tools of SFM to support a variety of companies and organizations, ranging from fresh start-ups to large multinational organizations with a long history.

It has been gratifying to witness this movement gather more and more momentum. There is now an international network of authorized SFM trainers, coaches and consultants. SFM seminars and certification programs are being given on every continent and SFM principles are being incorporated into the curricula of some of the world's top business schools.

As mentioned in our introductory section *About This Book*, this *Generative Consulting* book is the collaborative creation of my SFM Leadership Team – Colette, Kathrin, Jean-François, Elisabeth and Mickey. The *SFM Leadership Team* is a group of people who have been working intimately with me over the past five years to bring the vision and tools of Success Factor Modeling into world. The core team, which includes the authors and my older brother Michael Dilts, is also supported by our honorary members Gilles Roy, Magnus Kull, Nicolas von Burg and my wife Deborah Bacon Dilts.

The idea for this book was born during the first international Generative Consulting certification program that the SFM Leadership Team and I held at the University of California in Santa Cruz in August of 2018. Similar to the structure of the book, different SFM Leadership Team members have contributed to the design and delivery of the various application areas of the Generative Consulting program.

If you are interested in becoming a certified Generative Consultant and learning more about opportunities for authorization and affiliation with respect to generative consulting, please visit the *Dilts Strategy Group* website at: http://www.diltsstrategygroup.com

Certification in Generative Consulting, and in the other SFM areas of Next Generation Entrepreneur, Collective Intelligence and Conscious Leadership, qualify you for professional membership in the *International Association for Generative Change* (IAGC) as a *Practitioner of Generative Change in Business*. To learn more about IAGC and professional membership see: http://www.iagcglobal.com

In addition to consulting, training and writing, a key function of the SFM Leadership Team is to manage the three main "leaves" or areas of SFM activities:

* The *SFM Training Leaf* develops and delivers introductory programs and certification courses in Next Generation Entrepreneurship, Collective Intelligence, Conscious Leadership and Generative Consulting.

* The *SFM Consulting Leaf* supports organizations – from start-up ventures to multinational corporations – to identify their strengths and weaknesses and apply SFM tools and practices in order to reach a strong, sustainable and socially responsible state of growth and profitability.

* The *SFM Community Leaf* encourages dialog and collaborations within the SFM community. This leaf also includes an "SFM Meta Community" outreach that fosters connections, partnerships and projects between members of the SFM community and other communities, such as the International Association for Generative Change.

A core activity of the SFM Community Leaf is the *Generative Venture Circles* initiative. SFM Venture Circles are micro communities of SFM trained people who want to implement the Success Factor Modeling approach to identify and model the key success factors relating to a topic of common interest. Some current SFM modeling projects include:

* The *Success Factor Modeling for Healthcare* study, which is identifying the key success factors leading to effective healthcare within the larger healthcare ecosystem.

* The *SFM Corporate Social Responsibility and Sustainable Development* study, which seeks to identify the key goals, actions and qualities of mindset that characterize individuals, teams and ventures that are actively and effectively doing things to improve the environment and our quality of life on this planet.

* The *PERICEO Project* whose purpose is to foster synergy and increase Collective Intelligence in teams and organizations. In addition to a book, the project has resulted in an on-line Collective Intelligence assessment tool.

In addition to supporting such research studies, the SFM Community Leaf is planning a special SFM Crowdfunding platform to provide financial and other resources for SFM Venture Circle initiatives.

SFM Consulting Leaf activities include the development what we are calling the *SFM Venture Vitality Index* that ventures can use to assess their overall level of health and "fitness for the future."

As another SFM Consulting Leaf related activity, SFM Leadership Team member Mickey Feher and I have launched the *Success Mindset-Map Inventory* which has been featured as a key generative consulting tool in Chapters 2 and 5. You can find out more about how to become a member of the Success Mindset Coach Faculty and other opportunities for collaboration or partnership through *MindsetMaps International* at http://www.mindsetmaps.com

To find out more about all SFM activities and projects visit the Dilts Strategy Group website at http://www.diltsstrategygroup.com and subscribe to the *SFM Community Newsletter*. Through this newsletter you will learn about and be kept up-to-date on the activities taking place with respect to the three SFM leaves. For instance, you will get news about the latest Success Factor Modeling training programs being conducted around the world and how you can become an SFM coach, facilitator, consultant or authorized trainer.

As you can tell from what we have presented in this book, Success Factor Modeling is a dynamic and generative movement that is in a process of significant growth and expansion. I invite you to join us as we create a better future for ourselves, our planet and the generations to come.

Appendices

Appendix I: Generative Consulting Competences Scorecards

Systemic Thinking Skills

Ability to see how things fit into the bigger picture and work with multiple perspectives / truths

Systemic Thinking Skills Scorecard

Success Factor	Low Level						High Level
1. Acknowledging and Integrating Multiple Perspectives	*Speak primarily from one perspective or focus on single point of view*	1	2	3	4	5	*Include multiple views and different perspectives*
2. Keeping Connection to the Bigger Picture and Long-Term Consequences	*Focus on immediate issues and short-term results*	1	2	3	4	5	*Frequent reference to the bigger picture and long-term consequences*
3. Balancing Part and Whole	*Tendency to focus on either parts or the whole system*	1	2	3	4	5	*Include attention to both individual parts and the whole system*

Questions for self-reflection:

1. How many different perceptual positions did you acknowledge and include in your interactions?

2. How frequently did you make reference to and draw attention to the bigger picture and long-term consequences of the subject of your interactions?

3. Did you maintain a balance of attention between the individual parts and the whole system in your interactions?

Influencing Skills

Ability to persuade through presence congruence and alignment)

Influencing Skills Scorecard

Success Factor	Low Level						High Level
1. Maintaining a Generative State and a Focus on Shared Purpose and Creative Solutions	*Get lost or confused when others disagree or resist*	1	2	3	4	5	*Use a variety of methods to elicit and maintain a generative state and stay focused on the shared purpose of the conversation, seeking to find creative solutions*
2. Responding to the Positive Intention of Disagreements or Resistance	*Act aggressive or combative when others disagree or resist*	1	2	3	4	5	*Seek and respond to the positive intention behind the disagreement or resistance of others*
3. Providing a Larger and More Inclusive Perspective	*Rely primarily on verbal argumentation to support one point of view*	1	2	3	4	5	*Reframe disagreements and resistance as valuable insights into a more inclusive solution*

Questions for self-reflection:

1. Were you able to maintain a generative state in yourself and others during the interactions, irrespective of how smooth or challenging they were?

2. How effectively did you seek and respond to the positive intention behind disagreements or resistance?

3. Were you able to reframe disagreements and resistance as valuable insights for a more inclusive solution?

Emotional Intelligence

Ability to work with emotional states and to elicit emotional undercurrents (e.g., the shadow/"elephant in the room" no one is talking about)

Emotional Intelligence Scorecard

Success Factor	Low Level						High Level
1. Recognizing and Acknowledging Emotions	*Focus primarily on verbal content*	1	2	3	4	5	*Explicitly ask about and include feelings in all interactions*
2. Responding to Emotional Reactions with Equanimity	*Respond differently to various emotions arising in the interaction*	1	2	3	4	5	*Maintain a welcoming attitude (COACH State) for all emotional reactions, actively seeking out emotional undercurrents*
3. Welcoming and Making Space for Emotional Responses	*Seek only positive reactions*	1	2	3	4	5	*Verbally acknowledge and make space for all feelings, including difficult ones*

Questions for self-reflection:

1. How did you ensure to seek out and include feelings and emotional responses in your interactions?

2. How well were you able to identify and address any unspoken or hidden feelings or emotional reactions?

3. Did you verbally acknowledge and welcome all of the emotional responses that emerged during your interactions, including difficult feelings?

Facilitation Skills

Ability to recognize and support resonance and synergy between members of a group

Facilitation Skills Scorecard

Success Factor	Low Level						High Level
1. Keeping Focus on shared purpose	*Little reference is made to the shared outcomes of the group during interactions*	1	2	3	4	5	*Constantly draw attention to shared purpose during group interactions*
2. Finding and Creating Resonance	*Focus more attention to differences on a content level*	1	2	3	4	5	*Seek and point out similarities between group members in a variety of areas*
3. Identifying Synergy	*Strive for homogeneity and treat difference as a source of conflict and confusion*	1	2	3	4	5	*Help group members see how their differences complement each other in service of their shared purpose*
4. Promoting Emergence	*Rush to reach obvious conclusions*	1	2	3	4	5	*Give time, space and encouragement for something new to arise from interactions*

Questions for self-reflection:

1. How frequently did you draw attention to the shared purpose of the group during interactions?

2. How often and in how many different areas did you seek and point out similarities between group members?

3. Did differences between group members create conflict and confusion or were you able to guide the group to explore how their differences complement one another in service of their shared purpose?

4. How much time, space and encouragement did you give for something new and unexpected to arise out of the group interaction?

Communication Skills

Fluency in talking to different types and levels of people

Communication Skills Scorecard

Success Factor	Low Level						High Level
1. Reaching Different Types and Levels of People	*Primarily direct messages to one type or level of people*	1	2	3	4	5	*Adapt and direct messages to all of types and levels of people involved in the interaction*
2. Using Both Verbal and Non-Verbal Modalities	*Focus mainly on verbal content*	1	2	3	4	5	*Attend to and use many accompanying non-verbal messages*
3. Responding to Feedback	*Ignore feedback or fail to calibrate adequately*	1	2	3	4	5	*Perceive and respond quickly to both verbal and non-verbal feedback*
4. Using Verbal Reframing to Present and Draw Attention to New Perspectives	*Few attempts to present new or different perspectives*	1	2	3	4	5	*Use verbal reframing to bring new perspectives to the situations being discussed*

Questions for self-reflection:

1. Did you adapt your communication style in order to address all of types and levels of people involved in the interaction?

2. How much did you use non-verbal as well as verbal communication during your interactions?

3. How quickly were able to perceive and respond to both verbal and non-verbal feedback?

4. How often did you use verbal reframing to bring new perspectives to the situations being discussed?

Presentation Skills

Ability to speak to an audience using multiple communication channels (verbal, visual, metaphorical, somatic, etc.)

Presentation Skills Scorecard

Success Factor	Low Level						High Level
1. Using Verbal Language Appropriately and Impactfully	Too much or confusing use of language	1	2	3	4	5	Clear and helpful use of words
2. Using Visual Images and Diagrams Appropriately and Impactfully	Use few images or images that do not support or add to the message	1	2	3	4	5	Use images that support clearer and better understanding of the message
3. Using Metaphors Appropriately and Impactfully	Use few or irrelevant metaphors	1	2	3	4	5	Use metaphors that help to deepen the understanding of the message
4. Using Somatic Gestures Appropriately and Impactfully	Use few or misleading gestures and unrelated somatic expressions	1	2	3	4	5	Use gestures and other somatic expressions that help to keep attention and promote understanding

Questions for self-reflection:

1. How clear and helpful was your use of verbal language?

2. Did you use images that supported a clearer and better understanding of your message?

3. Did you use metaphors that helped to deepen the understanding of your message?

4. How often did you use non-verbal communication skills (spatial anchoring, gestures, somatic expressions) to help keep attention and promote a better understanding of your message?

Relational Skills

Ability to establish rapport and create trust

Relational Skills Scorecard

Success Factor	Low Level						High Level
1. Giving Time and Attention to Building Trust and Creating an Environment of Psychological Safety	*Focus is mainly on tasks and transactional activities*	1	2	3	4	5	*Significant attention and energy are put into building rapport and trust*
2. Identifying and Mirroring Back Important Issues.	*Minimal acknowledgment of client's key concerns and input*	1	2	3	4	5	*Ongoing acknowledgment and feeding back of client's issues and ideas*
3. Adapting Vocabulary and Pace to Match that of the Client	*Primarily use own vocabulary and timing*	1	2	3	4	5	*Adjust wording and timing to fit the client*

Questions for self-reflection:

1. What did you do to build trust and create an environment of psychological safety with your client?

2. How frequently did you acknowledge your client's feedback, concerns and ideas?

3. In what way did you adjust your language and timing to pace and match that of your client?

Pattern Detection Skills

Ability to spot both strong and weak signals on different levels of trends and meaning in data and interpersonal interactions

Pattern Detection Skills Scorecard

Success Factor	Low Level						High Level
1. Perceiving Multiple Levels of Trends (environment, behavior, capabilities, values and beliefs, identity and purpose)	*Focus on only a few levels of trends*	1	2	3	4	5	*Look for patterns at all levels*
2. Finding Patterns in Both Data and Personal Interactions	*Focus on a single type of input*	1	2	3	4	5	*Interrelate patterns in both data and personal interactions (information and observation)*
3. Identifying and Attuning to Weak as Well as Strong Signals	*Focus only on obvious patterns*	1	2	3	4	5	*Alert and attentive to subtle information coming from many sources*

Questions for self-reflection:

1. On which levels (environment, behavior, capabilities, values and beliefs, identity and purpose) did you spot potential patterns and in regard to the SFM Circle of Success?

2. What kind of links did you make between information given and your personal observations?

3. How did you integrate different levels of information coming from data, the business ecosystem and interpersonal interactions to find key patterns?

Strategic Thinking Skills

Ability to work on both ambition and vision (meaning and purpose) and see how smaller steps create a critical path to a larger outcome

Strategic Thinking Skills Scorecard

Success Factor	Low Level						High Level
1. Perceiving and Defining a Critical Path	*Focus on short-term goals and objectives*	1	2	3	4	5	*Bring attention to how next steps relate to moving in the direction of the bigger picture*
2. Balancing Ambition and Vision	*Vision and ambition are treated separately*	1	2	3	4	5	*Ambitions are seen in relation to the larger vision and kept in balance*
3. Chunking Up and Down	*Tendency to focus primarily on either details of generalities*	1	2	3	4	5	*Attend to both details and generalities, referencing how they relate to one another*

Questions for self-reflection:

1. How did you ensure that your client is not only focusing on the next steps (short-term objectives) but also keeping consistent attention on the bigger picture (longer-term direction)?

2. How did you ensure that Ambitions were aligned with the larger Vision?

3. How did you use both details and knowledge about the bigger picture to build a critical path leading to both the ambition and the vision?

Appendix II: MailNinja's growth success story

The roadmap to success through the application of the SFM models

Tony Nutley

CEO & Founder of the UK College of Personal Development

COO & Co-Founder of MailNinja

Who is Tony Nutley?

His passion: making a difference in the world, empowering people to really figure things out and helping people be all they can be. He believes the power of personal development is miraculous.

> *I can help somebody with, any number of issues really, really quickly by following this very specific model and ask the right kind of questions... This is amazing!*

As a generative change leader, beyond being a CEO, COO, founder and co-founder of two successful businesses, Tony is also a trainer, consultant and executive coach.

What is SFM for Tony?

For Tony, SFM was a mind and mindset changing process, based on the track record of successful people using a model that could be applied to any kind of enterprise. Everything he learned from SFM was used to build, launch, grow and develop the UK College of Personal Development and the email agency MailNinja (www.mailninja.co.uk). The application of SFM Circle of Success and Generative Consulting DIAMOND Model have helped both of his businesses to adapt, morph and change to get through the ups, downs, and changes in the economy. The following example of how Tony built MailNMinja illustrates how he concrete applied these two models.

SFM is about building a successful business and creating solid ongoing, win-win relationships.

~ Tony Nutley

Where did MailNinja's success start?

 * Defining Present State: Gathering information and diagnosis of the current situation

 * Intention Setting: Establishing the desired state/direction for change

Fifteen years ago, his business partner Doug Dennison was working for a big corporation, one of the three biggest insurance companies in the world, and he hated it. He felt it was soul destroying and wanted to do something different. Tony inquired: *"Well, what do you want to do?"* Doug answered: ***"I want to do something that adds value to small businesses."*** That was the intention they started from. They explored some ideas, dreamed up what they were going to do and decided they would be an ESP – Email Service Provider; an email marketing firm.

MailNinja overview

Started in 2005, in Swindon, UK with Doug Dennison CEO and Tony Nutley COO. In fifteen years, grew from nothing to 9 employees with a turnover of almost a million pounds a year

* **Vision:** To add value to small to medium sized businesses and help them grow much bigger

* **Mission:** To be an Email Service Provider and do email marketing. To support people who use MailChimp as their preferred ESP.

* **Ambition:** To be the number one email service supporter in the UK and have a worldwide customer base, sending out millions of emails and a million and a half-ton of business by the end of the year 2020.

* **Milestones:** Partnering with the biggest ESP email service provider in the world – MailChimp

* **Means to succeed:** Guided by SFM and what he learned from Robert and his late brother John Dilts.

What did MailNinja do to succeed?

 * **A**ction Planning: Building a critical path

 * **M**oving to Action: Execution

Tony acted not just as a business owner, but also as a consultant; nudging, guiding and coaching where appropriate. His role involved supporting and mentoring Doug and the team where needed – to offer training, be a compass, keep it simple, making sure the culture was developing as they grew, and new people came on board. Through many one-on-one consultations and calls and a whiteboard, Tony and Doug used the SFM Circle of Success template both as an implicit and explicit guide. Beyond SFM, he says he also has three things *'tattooed on the inside of his eyelids'* when he works with people, three things he never forgets: Logical Levels, the S.C.O.R.E. Model and an outcome setting process (PESEO / APROCESS).

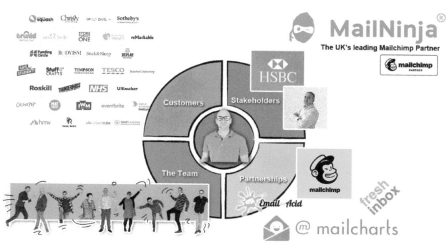

Vision: To add value to small-to medium-sized businesses and help them grow significantly.

Ambition: To be the number one Email Service Supporter in the U.K. and have a worldwide customer base, sending out millions of emails and making a million and a half-ton of business by the end of the year 2020.

Mission: To be an Email Service Provider and do email marketing; to support people who use MailChimp as their preferred ESP.

Role: To partner with the largest Email Service Provider (ESP) in the world – MailChimp

MailNinja- Circle of Success

MailNinja's Roadmap to success
How was the SFM Circle of Success applied?

1- *They built their SFM Circle of Success (CoS) with Doug being at the center of it all.*

* They explored- **Who** is this person was and what is his passion?

  Doug's passion is building business to helps business, do something that makes a difference and to do something that's his own.

* They determined- **How** we are going to enable that to happen along the logical levels?

  We looked into environment and capabilities, the Mission was clear, and we believed we could build this business.

* They identified-**Where** would be the gap that was going to cause them some pain.

  In the beginning, there was only Doug. And then we hired our first two apprentices.

  At first, we didn't have the bigger vision, we just wanted this to happen.

2- *Then they crystalized what kind of customer they wanted:*

* Small business to medium sized business owners and all marketing managers within slightly bigger enterprises.

3- *They identified who'd be the team they need and built it:*

* They had to hire people because they couldn't do it all themselves.

* They invested a huge amount of money in supporting their team members through training, development support and offsite initiatives.

4- *They found the stakeholders:*

* *HSBC, the bank became the biggest stakeholder because they fronted up some money for us, which was very nice of them to do that. Thanks very much HSBC.*

5- They found who they were going to partner with:

* They partnered with MailChimp, the biggest email service provider in the world, with whom they now have a fantastic win-win mutually supportive relationship.

* They also partnered with a couple of other key people and software organizations who were very supportive.

6- They planned and moved into action:

* They determined their vision and ambition.

We defined who we were as MailNinja: young, sprightly, fun, loving, interested in helping people grow their business. It's not just about the money, it's about adding value. These kinds of values have really guided us and helped us get where we are.

Where do we want to take this business and what's the ambition? Be number one in the UK and currently exploring a partnership which will lead to having an office in the USA. This will massively increase the turnover and the size of the team.

7- They transformed obstacles to stay on track, keep focus and stick to their plan:

* They made sure that there were regular checks and balances so that they did not lose their way.

We did have to step back and reassess: Who are we? Where we going? Is this what's important to us? Remember the original vision, who we are and our beliefs and values. Check for the gaps. Reassess.

E.g.: We hired somebody that was clearly a mistake as we lost sight of who we wanted to be, and what the actual vision was. We got far too bogged down in somebody else's outcome, about cash and chasing customers for the sake of chasing customers, even though some of them were the wrong customers. They weren't us and they were taking the business somewhere that just wasn't us. It was painful for us to recognize that the ego had taken over. Moreover, it wasn't our ego. It was somebody else who had joined as a business team member who decided to go in a direction that wasn't us. It wasn't our soul. They were creating something that they thought we wanted. And as much as it was great

*having more cash coming into the bank account, we asked
that person to leave the business because he wasn't who we
were. I don't want to be that kind of business. I don't think
that's long-term value adding, real value that is based on an
ethical win-win ongoing relationship. So that was very, very
clear to us about the ego part and the soul of who we are.*

*"Individuals, roles, teams, divisions and even an entire
organizational culture can be more "ego" oriented (security,
profit, ambition, etc) or more "soul" oriented (contribution,
service, vision, etc.). This affects what priorities are established
and how and which decisions are made. Ventures, new and old,
must constantly strive to maintain the balance between 'ego' and
'soul'. As companies grow and visions expands, it's ambition must
also be bigger. As a company increases its ambition, it's vision
must extend and broaden as well."*

Robert Dilts
*SFM Volume I:
Next Generation Entrepreneurs*

Other challenges met while growing and generative solutions found through some of the facets of the SFM DIAMOND model.

 * Obstacle Transformation: Dealing with challenges and pitfalls

1. Not having enough resource team members and necessary software engineers to police the Internet.

We paused and asked ourselves "Well, how else can we get
the necessary resources?" Interestingly, the guy who originally asked us for help was using MailChimp. And as his email
service provider, we approached them and said: "Hey, do you
have a partnership program?" They said yes. Today we've got
a very, very strong relationship MailChimp, which has been
a win-win thing for them and for us, because they see us
as a model agency and certainly their strongest UK partner.

2. Dealing with dips and what got us out of the dips

a. When you're in that dip, remember WHY you're doing in the first place.

b. Take time off, step back. Take a week off, get on an airplane and go sit in a hotel. Like the fish in the goldfish bowl, you can't see the water while swimming in it.

c. Reflect. Figure out what's gone wrong and how we can fix it. Then, think about, "Where are we going? What can we really do about the problem or the symptom?" Sometimes it's the economy and there's not much you can do about that. You have to rely on relationships and cut costs where you can, without being too brutal. But a lot of time it's because we've just lost sight of something because we've been so involved in the day to day grind.

How have things evolved? – MailNinja's passage from zero to hero.

 * Noting Progress: Assessing and measuring change

You could say the original idea of the vision was "drawn out on the back of a cigarette packet." I think North Americans say it was done on "a napkin in a coffee shop." That was the first time around, it was very loose. We have been building it up as we have gone along. Now, we are far more detail and evidence based with specific timelines and outcomes. We want this by this by such date, this is going to happen, and this is how we know it's going to be successful. We've got far more measurements that we didn't have our first time around.

What supports MailNinja's continued evolution and growth?

 * Deepening Practices: Follow up for deepening the changes

What were the necessary skills to hone or develop to continue growing? Tony shares 8 skills to be a successful entrepreneur and keep growing, and how they fit to our SFM DIAMOND Model:

1. Learn to **look in the mirror,** to be honest about what's important for us, and then how do we align the business with that. (Self-reflection).

2. Learn about **communicating a real sense of vision and mission** to the team and in an abstract way to potential customers and other people. (Communication and presentation skills)

   E.g. We've hired this new sales guy, Paul. He is fantastic. He is a professional guy and gets it straight away. He even understands what we don't want to become.

3. Learn to **negotiate with people** in a clear, uncomplicated way. Simplify business processes and contracts on one piece of paper, not pages and pages. "We will do this, you pay us that…" Simple! (Influencing skills)

4. Learn to **spot the right people** when hiring and **ask the right kind of questions.** (Systemic thinking)

5. Learn to keep your hand on the tiller, **steer the ship,** and not let somebody else drive the ship. Because the minute somebody else is driving the ship, they have their own destination in mind (Strategic thinking)

6. Learn to **keep channels open** and communication flowing. Be attuned and have those meetings every Monday to touch base with what's happening and make sure everything's on the right path. (Relational skills)

7. Learn to **support and empower** your team members. Learn how they want to be empowered. How can they be even more fantastic at their job? How can we support them to do amazing work? Whether it be a need for different computers, different software, some training, whatever it may be. (Emotional intelligence)

8. Learn to stay **generative and evolve** the vision, mission and ambition. We are launching a brand-new product that we've developed over the last year. It's another sort of step in the evolution of the business. We're not just a mail service provider, but now also software service provider. We saw what was going on in the marketplace, noticed customers wanted something slightly different, did some brainstorming and came up with an idea that could be useful. We validated proposal with customers. We tested it. We had to hire new people for that team. We now have an in-house developer who's been doing that for us. (Generative state)

Additional tips to next generation entrepreneurs:

* **Trust yourself.** If you really believe in something, test that it is not just in your head. Ask somebody, "Do you think this is a good idea?" And if you're clear about who your customers might be, ask some of them or people who are like them. Tell them, "I'm going to do this. Who's going to buy it?" Because there's no "best idea in the world'"in your head. If nobody wants it, what was the point? Check that somebody would want what you are imagining.

* **Get the best people around you** to help you because you can't do it all yourself. Don't be afraid to ask. You'd be surprised how willing people are to pitch in and help if you ask and they believe in what you're trying to do.

Appendix III: John's case study

This appendix introduces the detailed results of John's MindsetMap.

Meta Mindset

	Big Picture Clarity	Rating	John's Insights after coaching
	1.Know what you really love to do (Know what you are passionate about).	3	John had not thought about what his Passion was for many years. He did not see any connection between passion and work. He saw them as two unrelated areas and viewed his passion as something that should be practiced during his spare time. It was no surprise that he lacked the spark that ignites the fire of enthusiasm, determination and energy. His team felt that he had no drive.
	2. Know what you want to help create in the longer-term future (Are clear about your destination; and your longer-term vision)	5	John realized that he did not have a clear destination and vision in mind. He knew he was not satisfied with his current environment and the attitude of his bosses, but he was waiting for something to happen rather than going for what he truly wanted.
	3. Are clear about your direction, regardless of whether or not you know the ultimate destination.	9	John's knew the general direction he wanted to go. He was interested in sustainable energy projects.
	4. Know your purpose – know what you stand for and why you are doing what you are doing. .	5	This was a key area of development for John. During his coaching sessions, John created his purpose statement and reflected on his core values, which served as a compass for making decisions regarding his team and the future.
	6. Are clear about your ambition – what you want to become and achieve in the next two to five years.	9	John was very ambitious and knew he was destined to serve in an executive role and initially believed this meant taking over his boss's position. However, as he clarified his purpose and vision, he eventually realized that was not his path.
	7. Are clear about your role – the position you have with respect to others in your market/ environment.	9	John was relatively clear on this – however, he felt out of place in the company's culture and started to question whether his role was the right one.

228   Generative Consulting

Macro Mindset

Habits of Success	Rating	John's Insights after coaching
1. Doing what you are passionate about and investing a lot of energy and focus into making what you want happen.	4	John realized that, in his current position, he was forced to move to a more operational management role which was far from his passion of starting new things.
2. Seeking feedback and establishing ways to get honest and frequent feedback.	5	John realized that he was guessing a lot about what his superiors and peers thought about him; rather than having established channels for quality feedback from them.
3. Constantly scanning for opportunities and investing time to create them.	9	This was one of John's fortes.
4. Are internally grounded and resourceful and have your ways of recharging and balancing yourself and practice them on a daily basis.	5	There was much opportunity to do better in this area. As a result of receiving coaching, John restarted his yoga and meditation practice, which he had abandoned many years earlier.
5. Are aware of risks and potential problems and don't get discouraged or distracted in the face of adversity and negative feedback.	9	This was another one of John's fortes. However, with an unclear vision, it resulted in a type of perseverance that required an excessive amount of energy from John, rather than "a flexible dance with forces."

Micro Mindset

Put an "√" in the columns that most fit for you with respect to the following actions

Action	I enjoy it	I am good at it	I am spending time doing it
1. Setting aside the time to explore and reconnect with what you love to do, what is important to you and what you are good at doing –i.e., your passion, your sense of purpose and your excellence.	√	√	No
2. Creating opportunities for ongoing dialog with customers and prospects.	√	√	√
3. Brainstorming and implementing products and services that anticipate and fulfill customer needs.	√	√	No
4. Attracting and providing direction and support to team members and encouraging team cooperation.	√	√	No
5. Encouraging team members and providing them with opportunities to learn and grow.	√	√	√
6. Identifying potential investors and providers of other essential resources and creatively securing their interest and commitment to support your venture.	√	√	√
7. Creating and developing a sustainable infrastructure and a path to growth and scalability for your venture.	√	√	√
8. Seeking and establishing win-win relationships with potential partners and allies who resonate with your values and vision.	√	√	√
9. Identifying and leveraging synergies between what you are doing and the products, services or competences of other ventures.	√	√	√

As these results indicate, John enjoyed and was good at almost all of these actions. He did not, however, spend enough time to:

* explore and reconnect with his passion, his sense of purpose and his area of excellence.
* brainstorm and implement products and services that anticipated and fulfilled customer needs.
* attract and provide direction and support to team members, and encourage team cooperation.

Meta Goal

John's current focus was:

"To Increase My Personal Satisfaction in what I am doing"

**Increase
Personal
Satisfaction**

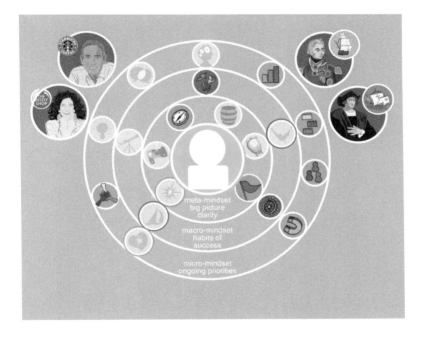

Given John's goal to increase his personal satisfaction in what he was doing, his MindsetMap results are shown above. The full color icons show areas of high self-rating. The icons circled in red show the most important areas for improvement in order for John to achieve his meta goal.

You can take the Success MindsetMap Inventory yourself, free of charge at
www.mindset-maps.com.

Bibliography

1 - Overview of Generative Consulting

Books

* Dilts, Robert; *From Coach to Awakener*, Dilts Strategy Group, 2003, 2018.

* Dilts, Robert; *Success Factor Modeling, Vol. I: Next Generation Entrepreneurs – Live Your Dream and Make a Better World Through Your Business*, Dilts Strategy Group, 2015.

* Dilts, Robert; *Success Factor Modeling, Vol. II: Generative Collaboration – Releasing the Creative Power of Collective Intelligence*, Dilts Strategy Group, 2016.

* Dilts, Robert; *Success Factor Modeling, Volume III – Conscious Leadership and Resilience: Orchestrating Innovation and Fitness for the Future*, Dilts Strategy Group, 2017.

* Dilts, R. and DeLozier, J. with Bacon Dilts, D., *NLP II: The Next Generation*, Dilts Strategy Group, 2010, 2018.

* Koestler, Arthur, *Act of Creation*, Penguin Books, 1964.

* Wilber, Ken, *A Brief History of Everything*, Shambhala Publications, 1996.

2 - Managing Growth in Business

Books

* Dilts, Robert; *Success Factor Modeling, Vol. I: Next Generation Entrepreneurs – Live Your Dream and Make a Better World Through Your Business*, Dilts Strategy Group, 2015.

* Dilts, Robert - *Law of Requisite Variety*, NLP University Press, 1998.

Online resources

* CNW Telbec, *Cascades recognized for its responsible best practices* https://www.newswire.ca/news-releases/cascades-recognized-for-its-responsible-best-practices-890166687.html

* Mansfield, Matt. *STARTUP STATISTICS – The Numbers You Need to Know*. https://smallbiztrends.com/2019/03/startup-statistics-small-business.html

* Otar, Chad. *What Percentage Of Small Businesses Fail -- And How Can You Avoid Being One Of Them?* https://www.forbes.com/sites/forbesfinancecouncil/2018/10/25/what-percentage-of-small-businesses-fail-and-how-can-you-avoid-being-one-of-them/#2722e18643b5

3 - How to Generatively Manage Crisis in Business

Books:

* Pink, Daniel H.; *Drive: The surprising truth about what motivates us*. Riverhead Books, 2009.

* Dilts, *Robert; Success Factor Modeling, Volume III – Conscious Leadership and Resilience: Orchestrating Innovation and Fitness for the Future*, Dilts Strategy Group, 2017.

* Mihaly Csikszentmihalyi. *Good Business: leadership, flow and the making of meaning*. Penguin Books, 2004.

Articles :

* Hershatter, Andrea; Epstein, *Molly: Millennials and the World of Work: An Organization and Management Perspective*, Journal of Business and Psychology, 25 (2): 211–223, 2010.

* Myers, K.; Sadaghiani, K. *Millennials in the Workplace: A Communication Perspective on Millennials, Organizational Relationships and Performance*, Journal of Business and Psychology. 25 (2): 225–238, 2010.

Online resource :

* Khurana, R., Nohria, N., *Hippocratic path for managers* 2008 HBR 86 no. 10, 70-77 https://hbr.org/2008/10/its-time-to-make-management-a-true-profession

* Wikipedia : *https://en.wikipedia.org/wiki/Crisis*

4 - How to best Manage Transition in Business

Books :

* Bridges, William, *Managing Transitions : Making the Most of Change*, Perseus Publishing, 2003

* Deaton, Ann V., *VUCA Tools for a VUCA World: Developing Leaders and Teams for Sustainable Results*, Da Vinci Resources, 2018

* Dilts, Robert; *Success Factor Modeling, Vol. II: Generative Collaboration – Releasing the Creative Power of Collective Intelligence*, Dilts Strategy Group, 2016.

* Dilts R., Falcone E., Meiss I., Roy G., *The PERICEO TOOL- « Teams and Organizations, develop your capacity for Collective Intelligence* – Dilts Strategy Group, 2018

5 - A practical Approach - How does it all come together?

Books :

* Dilts, Robert; *Success Factor Modeling, Volume III – Conscious Leadership and Resilience: Orchestrating Innovation and Fitness for the Future*, Dilts Strategy Group, 2017.

* Hofstede, Geert *Culture's Consequences: comparing values, behaviors, institutions, and organizations across nations* (2nd ed.). SAGE Publications. 2001.

Online resources :

* Cone Communications LLC, 2016 *Cone Communications Millennial Employee Engagement Study* https://www.conecomm.com/research-blog/2016-millennial-employee-engagement-study

* David Gelles D. , Yaffe-Bellany, D. *Shareholder Value Is No Longer Everything, Top C.E.O.s Say* https://www.nytimes.com/2019/08/19/business/business-roundtable-ceos-corporations.html

* Friedman Fulton, *A Friedman doctrine - The Social Responsibility Of Business Is to Increase Its Profits* https://www.nytimes.com/1970/09/13/archives/a-friedman-doctrine-the-social-responsibility-of-business-is-to.html

* Imperative Group, *Workforce Purpose Index and Make Work More Meaningful* https://www.imperative.com/research

* LinkedIn, *Workplace Culture Trends: The Key to Hiring (and Keeping) Top Talent in 2018* https://blog.linkedin.com/2018/june/26/workplace-culture-trends-the-key-to-hiring-and-keeping-top-talent

* MindsetMaps International, https://www.mindset-maps.com

* Noble, Holcomb B., *Dr. Viktor E. Frankl of Vienna, Psychiatrist of the Search for Meaning, Dies at 92*, https://www.nytimes.com/1997/09/04/world/dr-viktor-e-frankl-of-vienna-psychiatrist-of-the-search-for-meaning-dies-at-92.html

About the Authors

Robert B. Dilts has had a global reputation as a leading coach, behavioral skills trainer and business consultant since the late 1970s. A major developer and expert in the field of Neuro-Linguistic Programming (NLP), Robert has provided coaching, consulting and training throughout the world to a wide variety of individuals and organizations.

Together with his late brother John, Robert pioneered the principles and techniques of Success Factor Modeling™ and has authored numerous books and articles about how they may be applied to enhance leadership, creativity, communication and team development. In addition to Robert's three volume series on *Success Factor Modeling*, his book *Visionary Leadership Skills* draws from his extensive study of historical and corporate leaders to present the tools and skills necessary for "creating a world to which people want to belong." *Alpha Leadership: Tools for Business Leaders Who Want More From Life* (with Ann Deering and Julian Russell) captures and shares best practices of effective leadership, offering approaches to reduce stress and to promote satisfaction. *From Coach to Awakener* provides a road map and set of toolboxes for coaches to help clients reach goals on a number of different levels of learning and change. *The Hero's Journey: A Voyage of Self Discovery* (with Stephen Gilligan) is about how to reconnect with your deepest calling, transform limiting beliefs and habits and improve self-image.

Past corporate clients and sponsors include Apple Computer, Microsoft, Hewlett-Packard, IBM, Lucasfilms Ltd. and the State Railway of Italy. He has lectured extensively on coaching, leadership, innovation, collective intelligence, organizational learning and change management, making presentations and keynote addresses for The International Coaching Federation (ICF), HEC Paris, The United Nations, The World Health Organization, Harvard University and the International University of Monaco. In 1997 and 1998, Robert supervised the design of *Tools for Living*, the behavior management portion of the program used by Weight Watcher's International.

Robert was an associate professor at the ISVOR Fiat School of Management (the former corporate university of the Fiat Group) for more than fifteen years, helping to develop programs on leadership, innovation, values and systemic thinking. From 2001–2004 he served as chief scientist and Chairman of the Board for ISVOR DILTS Leadership Systems, a joint venture with ISVOR Fiat that delivered a wide range of innovative leadership development programs to corporations on a global scale.

A co-founder of Dilts Strategy Group, Robert was also founder and CEO of Behavioral Engineering, a company that developed computer software and hardware applications emphasizing behavioral change. Robert has a degree in Behavioral Technology from the University of California at Santa Cruz.

Elisabeth Falcone lives in the south of France and works internationally as a generative coach, consultant, facilitator and master trainer in NLP. She is part of the Dilts Strategy Group leadership team and co-author of *The PERICEO Tool: Teams and organizations, develop Your capacity for collective intelligence* with Robert Dilts, Gilles Roy and Isabelle Meiss. She developed the PERICEO Team Profile and trains and certifies consultants in its use (www.periceo.com).

Elisabeth began her career as a management controller in national and international groups, which enabled her to understand the global functioning of organizations and the various "levers and brakes" involved.

She has always been passionate about creating bridges between individuals and cultures, the humanities, social sciences and neurosciences, and from very early on she has worked in sectors with a high level of diversity - intercultural, generational, gender equality, disability, etc.

Convinced that the greatest wealth and fragility of any organization is its human capital, she has created a global approach for both individuals and the groups they are part of, "Towards the best version of yourself," to help them boost their performance and achieve their calling.

Contributing to this book, belonging to this team and meeting as many wonderful people like YOU is a wonderful "unexpected journey": infinite gratitude!

For more visit :

www.intelligencecollective-coaching-pnl.com

www.verslameilleureversiondesoi.com

www.periceo.com

Contact Elisabeth : ef@intelligencecollective-coaching-pnl.com

Mickey A Feher is Hungarian-American based in New York who works internationally as a generative consultant, facilitator and coach. He has been the Managing Director and Sales Director at major multinational companies such as Deutsche Telekom, Aegis and Deloitte and served in various executive level roles across Europe.

His passion includes working with men to redefine healthy masculinity in all roles men play in life and he founded the MANTORHSIFT Initiative and the MANTORSHIFT Podcast to advance this mission.

He is also the co-founder of MindsetMaps International with Robert Dilts and the co-creator of the Success MindsetMap™ Inventory illustrated by Antonio Meza. He is the CEO of Purpose & Company, an international organizational development company active in both Europe and the US. Previously he served as the Executive Director for The International Association for Generative Change, a global organization founded by Robert Dilts and Steve Gilligan. He is an active member of the leadership team of the Dilts Strategy Group. His passion and higher purpose is to help others find meaning in their life and reach exceptional results. He is engaged in a lifelong battle against isolationism, intolerance and hatred.

Mickey's clients include some the largest multinationals of the world such as Microsoft; GE; Vodafone and Mondelez as well as EDF, and also workes with small and medium size enterprises and entrepreneurs. He has an MA in psychology and MBA in international management from Case Western University and is Master Practitioner; Consultant and Trainer certified by NLP University. He is also a Generative Coach certified by the IAGC and is a qualified trainer of SFM1 and SFM3. He is a father of two who practices martial arts, yoga and meditation every day.

For more visit

www.mantorshift.com

www.purposeandcompany.com

Contact Mickey: office@mindsetmaps.com

Colette Normandeau is an international NLP Master-trainer, SFM I, II and III facilitator, generative consultant and certified executive and life NLP coach. She is a member of the Dilts Strategy Group Leadership Team.

Colette is the founder of L'essentiel, an international NLP training school based in Quebec City, Canada dedicated in training and certifying Life, Business and Executive NLP coaches.

Since 2001, Colette has been living her passion and mission of supporting, through training, conferences, coaching and consulting, thousands of entrepreneurs, teams, managers, leaders, businesses in Canada, France, Morocco, Mexico, the USA, the UK, and Finland. Her clients are people of influence who want to make a positive difference in their lives, in the lives of others and in the world. She is the author of best-selling 2011 French book *Ê.T.R.E. enfin soi-même*, a self-coaching guide to BEING yourself and awakening. Inspired by a vision she had during an SFM exercise in Santa Cruz in 2016 for the future of NLP and our world, she initiated, in 2017, the first NLP 4th generation co-creation movement in Bali. The sprouting movement now has research & development cells starting in many areas of the world. She is one of three nominees in the "Business Category" at the London ANLP 2020/2021 awards. Colette strives to support leaders in becoming more aligned and connected in their Being, empowered to succeed in business and in life and leading daily in a more conscious, creative and Heart-Based way. She loves to see people and business's shine and thrive, through the awakening of their generativity and spiritual intelligence.

For more visit:

www.ecolepnl.com

www.colettenormandeau.com

www.nlp4thgeneration.com

www.unleashinghbl.com

Jean-François Thiriet lives with his family in Besançon on the eastern part of France. At age 48, he is now the developer of the Generative Mastermind Model and the MBA index that help people successfully launch their generative mastermind groups.

His vision of mastermind groups – *a mastermind group for all, and for each, a mastermind group* – has lead him to create the Mastermind Business Academy that delivers online, worldwide trainings for coaches, trainers and consultants who want to certify themselves as master facilitators.

He is a founding member of the Dilts Strategy Group SFM Leadership Team and is trained and certified in SFM1 *Next Generation Entrepreneur*, SFM2 *Generative Collaboration*, SFM3 *Conscious Leadership* and is a Generative Consulting trainer.

Jean François is also trained and certified as a coaching supervisor, collective intelligence facilitator, mediator and executive coach.

As a facilitator, he uses body , metaphorical and emotional intelligence in his workshops to help his clients think out of the box of their cognitive mind, something he has learned from his martial arts practice and from his mentors for 30 years

He is very grateful to Robert Dilts and the Dilts Strategy Group for this opportunity to contribute to this book.

For more visit:

www.coaching-facilitation.fr

www.partagetongenie.fr

Contact Jean-François: jft@coaching-facilitation.fr

Kathrin M. Wyss, M.S. Pharm, B.A.Com

Kathrin, born in Switzerland, founded her coaching and training company Beachtig CTC in 2004, and since 2008 has worked full-time internationally as an Executive Coach, Leadership Trainer, and Change Agent. She is a founding member of the Dilts Strategy Group SFM Leadership team, a co-facilitator and trainer for all SFM trainings and a vital contributor to the first training of Generative Consulting in 2019. She is also a Fellow Trainer in NLP, a Shamanic Practitioner and a long-term Zen pupil, which shapes her unique holistic approach.

She began her professional career as a pharmacist and spent more than a decade in the international healthcare industry and the Swiss government healthcare system in several management positions. She is a highly versatile, accomplished and passionate person who knows how to break down cognitive knowledge into daily tasks, to inspire other people and to achieve sustainable change. She acts as a catalyst for individuals and teams to gain key insights, greater clarity and overall alignment of their visions as professionals, teams and as human beings. Kathrin 's clients include top Fortune 500 companies, executives from C-Suite and VP-level as well as conscious entrepreneurs and leaders.

For more please visit:

www.beachtig.com

www.linkedin.com/in/beachtig

Contact Kathrin: office@beachtig.com

Antonio Meza is an architect of vision, supporting entrepreneurs and leaders around the world to communicate complex ideas in a simple and fun way through illustrations, cartoons, or through structuring presentations, books, or websites.

A native of Pachuca, Mexico, Antonio is a Master Practitioner and a Trainer of Neuro-Linguistic Programming (NLP). He has a degree in Communication Sciences from Fundación Universidad de las Américas Puebla, a Masters degree in Film Studies from Université de Paris 3 –Sorbonne Nouvelle, a diploma in Cinema Scriptwriting from the General Society of Writers in Mexico (SOGEM), and a diploma in Documentary Films from France's École Nationale des Métiers de l'Image et du Son (La Fémis). He is also certified in the three levels of the SFM system.

He worked in Mexico as a freelance filmmaker and participated in animated cartoons startups before moving to France where he works as a consultant, coach, and trainer, specializing in storytelling, creative thinking and collective intelligence.

Antonio is also an experienced public speaker member of Toastmasters International. In 2015 he was awarded best speaker at the International Speech Contest of District 59, covering South-West Europe, and reached the semifinals at international level.

He has illustrated 10 books including the 3 volumes of the *Success Factor Modeling* series with Robert Dilts, the *Mastermind Groups* book and the *PERICEO Tool* for Dilts Strategy Group.

He also uses his skills as a cartoonist and trainer to collaborate in seminars, conferences and brainstorming sessions as a graphic facilitator, and to produce animated videos to explain complex information in a clear and fun way.

Antonio lives in Paris with his wife Susanne, his daughter Luz Carmen and his cats Ronja and Atreju.

For more visit:

www.antoons.net

www.linkedin.com/in/antoniomeza/

Contact Antonio: hola@antoons.net

CPSIA information can be obtained
at www.ICGtesting.com
Printed in the USA
BVHW020605221020
591491BV00030B/536